GHOST ROCK

Joe Josephson, Chris Perry & Andy Genereux

to Margo, Darlene & Carolyn

Rocky Mountain Books

GHOST ROCK

Joe Josephson, Chris Perry & Andy Genereux

Front cover: Dwayne Congdon on the memorable pitch two of "The Wraith." Photo: Grant Statham.
Back cover: Sport climbing on the Arrowhead in Devil's Gap. Photo: Paul Valiulis.
Title page: Some people call him the Fred Beckey of the Ghost. We refer to Fred as the Frank Campbell of everything non-Ghost. Frank on pitch two on the second ascent of "The Separated Reality." Photo: Joe Josephson.

Photo credits not otherwise acknowledged:
Chris Perry: 22.1, 22.2, 32, 33, 35, 37, 40, 44, 46, 54, 56, 59, 60, 68, 82, 101, 109, 114, 118, 136, 146, 152, 154, 156, 158, 171, 173, 180, 201, 204, 207, 210, 215, 220, 222, 223, 228, 230.
Joe Josephson: 23.2, 25.1, 25.2, 39, 47, 49, 52, 62, 93, 182, 189, 209.
Andy Genereux: 6, 24.1, 24.2, 27.1, 74, 138, 163, 231.
Frank Campbell: 219, 217, 221. Jon Jones: 197, 199. CMC History by Chic Scott: 23.1, 24.3.
Trevor Jones: 21. Brad Wrobleski: 148.

Copyright © 1997 Joe Josephson, Chris Perry, Andy Genereux

All rights reserved. No part of this book
may be reproduced in any form without
permission in writing from the publisher,
except by a reviewer who may quote brief
passages in a review.

The publisher gratefully acknowledges the assistance
provided by the Alberta Foundation for the Arts and by
the federal Department of Communications.

COMMITTED TO THE DEVELOPMENT OF CULTURE AND THE ARTS

Published by Rocky Mountain Books
#4 Spruce Centre SW, Calgary, AB T3C 3B3
Printed and bound in Canada by
RMB Hignell Book Printing Ltd., Winnipeg

Canadian Cataloguing in Publication Data

Josephson, Joe, 1967-
  Ghost rock

  ISBN 0-921102-61-5

  1. Rock climbing--Alberta--Ghost River Valley--Guidebooks.
2. Rock climbing--Alberta--Waiparous River Valley--
Guidebooks. 3. Ghost River Valley (Alta.)--Guidebooks. 4.
Waiparous River Valley (Alta.)--Guidebooks. I. Perry, Chris,
1945- II. Genereux, Andy, 1959- III. Title.
GV199.44.C22A4575 1997   796.5'223'09712332   C97-910546-3

TABLE OF CONTENTS

Introduction

Introduction—7
Type of Climbing—9
Hazards—13
The Three R's—15

Getting There—17
Camping—19
History—21
Using this Guide—28

The Climbs

Orient Point—31

Devil's Gap—35

Planters Valley—37
Spectre Crag—55
Wild West Wall—63
Kemp Shield—69
Bonanza Area—75
Grey Ghost Wall—83
Epitaph Wall—95
Spirit Pillar—102
Phantom Tower—109
Border Bluffs—118
Kolbassa Wall—136
Morning Glory Tower—142

Ghost River Valley—145

South Phantom Crag—147
Montana Buttress—149

North Phantom Crag—154
Wully Canyon—170
Wully Wall—172
Sentinel Bluffs—183
Sentinel Crag—188

North Ghost Valley—194

Sunset Boulevard—195
Alberta Jam—199
Silver-Tongued Devil Crag—203
Bastion Wall—208

Waiparous Creek—215

Sunrise Wall—216
Pinto Wall—220
The Prow—222

The Anti-Ghost—223

Alpine Rock—227

Maps

General Access—16
Devil's Gap—30

Ghost River Valley—144
Waiparous Creek—214

Access Note

The Ghost is a special place. It has long been considered a quiet, adventurous and even spiritual place to explore. Part of the pleasure of the Ghost is the virtually unrestricted access for much of the area (except for Banff National Park and the Ghost River Wilderness). This may also become the Ghost's downfall. Utility workers, oil and gas companies, abuse-rehab programs, family campers, four-wheelers, motocross riders, native groups, the military, hunters and climbers have all run roughshod over the Ghost landscape year round. For the most part, this has historically been a very congenial and respectful co-existence. It would be naive, however, to expect that the present state of affairs will not change. If the road is somehow miraculously upgraded or worse, closed. If the wrong, politically-connected person gets ahold of land rights and services like toilets and campgrounds get established, or if a myriad of other developmental nightmares get started, the Ghost will undoubtedly be the scene of an ugly fight. We believe it is important for us as climbers to establish a strong and respectful stakehold in the future of the Ghost. It seems consensus that most people that use the Ghost (including non-climbers) do not want to see the present status change too much. Therefore it is extremely important that we all treat the area well, not be obnoxious or pester other visitors, respect the national park and forest service regulations, not make a mess of the campsites (or worse, burn the area down), and not harass wildlife or otherwise destroy the fragile ecosystem.

INTRODUCTION

Numerous features come to a dramatic union in the Ghost River to produce a most unique and unforgettable rock climbing arena. There are over 200 kilometres of steep cliff line in the region. In June and July when the wildflowers are in bloom, it is simply beautiful. Plus, the remote and relatively wild nature of the Ghost Valley adds a strong adventure component that has as much to do with the climbing as the routes themselves. There are no highways or railroads visible from the Ghost. Aside from the occasional small airplane flying through Devil's Gap or the whine of ATVs, you will be left alone to the sounds of wind, rivers and your partner(s).

By local standards, the Ghost has climbing on above-average rock. To date, however, it is woefully underdeveloped. Although the Ghost has one of the longest climbing histories in the area, it would be fair to claim that the present state of development is in the same position the Bow Valley was in some 10-12 years ago.

The abundant crags that make up the Ghost River rock climbing are only a small part of the mountains found there. For those inclined, there are several alpine rock climbs described beginning on page 227.

Included in this book is a chapter on the rock climbs of Waiparous Creek beginning on page 214.

The Waiparous Creek area lies to the north of Black Rock Mountain, and along with its tributaries, is pretty much the most northerly extension of the Ghost's dramatic cliff lines. It is, however, considered a totally separate venue because getting there makes the rest of the Ghost seem casual. Frank Campbell is, to date, the only regular climber to tap into the vast resource of quality limestone found there. The authors are eternally grateful to Frank for divulging what has been for years his "secret" spot. The information given here is strictly to catalogue what has been done, present an introduction to the area and foster dreams of adventure. However the information is not conclusive or guaranteed to be accurate. And until the access improves, the area gets more visits, or more climbs are completed we leave it for your own discovery.

Acknowledgements

The authors are indebted to the support and information from the following individuals: Jon Jones and John Martin for use of information and topos from *Sport Climbs in the Canadian Rockies (1996)*. A huge slap on the back goes out to longtime Ghost pioneers Dave Morgan, Trevor Jones and Frank Campbell for sharing their routes, photos and stories (buy them a beer when you see them!). We appreciate Glen Boles for permission to reproduce information from his venerable, green guide *Rocky Mountains of Canada South*. Others who have assisted in providing information and photographs are: Don Vockeroth, Paul Stoliker, Chas Yonge, Andy Skuce, John Rowe, Tim Pochay, Paul Valiulis, Grant Statham, Dale Bartrom, Keith Haberl, Albi Sole, Geoff Powter, Al Pickel, The Calgary Mountain Club World News and the Sherwood House in Canmore.

TYPE OF CLIMBING

All of the routes in this book are on limestone. Most of the Ghost River climbing is on Eldon Formation, which is the same as Yamnuska. (The other formation present is Cathedral-Phantom Bluffs.) As a result, the climbing is similar to that on Yam and mainly follows steep crack lines. Overall, though, the rock is better than the Bow Valley and in many cases it is exceptional. Alongside the crack lines there are vast quantities of sweeping, compact, waterworn walls that have begun to produce some fine, if not prickly, face climbs. The better climbing tends to start in the moderately hard grades (5.9 and up), although there are a number of quality 5.7s to 5.8s. Beware that the rock can be brittle and seemingly solid holds have on occasion been known to snap with little warning. Keep this fact clearly in mind when attempting new routes or soloing. As well, most ledges will be scree covered and it is therefore advisable to wear a helmet. Rough-jagged cracks, textured arêtes, bulging walls, razor-sharp ripples and square edges combine throughout the Ghost to produce what is, arguably, the best limestone climbing in the Canadian Rockies. To date, all of the climbing has been on walls varying from slabs to slightly overhanging and ranging in length from 15 to 360 metres. See the individual chapters for the specifics on each cliff.

Gear

Unlike most local limestone areas, the Ghost is blessed with a lion's share of great crack climbs making camming units and wired nuts desireable. One can come to the Ghost with nothing but a rack of quick draws but you will miss out on major portions of what the Ghost has to offer. Every effort has been made to determine if a route requires the use of pitons. If in doubt, particularly on the older, obscure climbs, a selection of 4-6 pins up to a 1/2" angle will usually suffice.

A standard rack would include a set of wires, a full set of camming units including a few smaller "TCUs," and a few Tri-cams™ and/or Hexes depending upon your personal preferences. As well, efforts have been made to indicate if any unusually wide protection pieces are helpful.

As the camming units come in a variety of different models and changing preferences we have made no effort to translate from one brand of camming unit to another nor to measure the width of every crack. What you read is what we have been given by the contributing climbers or have personally experienced ourselves. If someone gave us Camalot™ sizes and all you have are Friends™ (or worse Hexcentrics™), then we leave it up to you to figure it out. None of the information is perfectly accurate and local limestone is notorious for accepting adequate protection for one party and none for another. Use your own judgment.

Ropes

Over the years the Ghost has been largely a traditional area. Even in this day of ultra-equipped sport routes many of the activists maintain some degree of

Waiparous Tower. Photo: Frank Campbell.

Type of Climbing

committment and adventure in their routes (This is the Ghost after all!). As a result, there are few areas where only one rope will suffice. Only one full-length route in the entire Ghost River is equipped for 25 m rappels—this is "Dirty Dancing" on North Phantom Crag. It is possible to descend from West Phantom Crag with one rope via the Bonanza Descent Gully but if the waterfall is flowing or you need to back off your route, you will be in trouble. Some of the big crags have walk-off descents but again, if you need to back off your route…. Most of the sport/cragging areas also require an extra rappel line. Be sure to check out all the details in the individual chapters before you commit yourself.

Note: Most multi-pitch routes do not have fixed belay or rappel anchors. If you need to back off such a route you will probably appreciate having a few pitons or extra wires/hexes along.

Fixed Protection

People have been climbing in the Ghost for over 25 years. As a result, the area has been influenced by various and widely different climbing styles. Many of the older routes have little or no fixed protection and if they do, they are typically pitons. Fixed pitons can loosen quickly in the local climate and/or may not have been well-placed to begin with. It is recommended to test all fixed pitons with a hammer before they are trusted. Do NOT test bolts with a hammer.

Some routes have bolts for belays and/or protection. Bolts on the older climbs (pre-1993) are pretty much all 5/16" self-drill concrete anchors with shear and pullout strength of about 2000 kg. On these, you will find a variety of hangers. They range from homemade aluminum (up to the late eighties) to homemade steel and modern stainless steel brands. Note that on some of the older cragging routes at Kemp Shield and Sentinel Bluffs the homemade hangers have exceptionally small carabiner holes (0.5" diameter). A selection of small profile carabiners is required. Otherwise you can feed a wired nut through the hole and clip the wire so the nut jams against the hanger. Beware that it is unknown whether this procedure affects the strength of the hanger or the wire.

To date, the authors have not heard of a 5/16" self-drive bolt failing. Although there are no formal tests or accounts of failures, it seems the bolts themselves are fine but it is the cap screw that presents the weakest link. In the early days they were plain steel screws with Allen-key heads. These are susceptible to rust and should be replaced with newer case-hardened, aircraft-quality cap screws (identified by the star pattern on the head). Unfortunately, these older screws most often break while attempting to unscrew them. If this is the case the entire bolt should be replaced.

Note: Virtually every pre-1996 self-drive bolt is on imperial threads. The 5/16" imperial Rawl bolt is no longer made and it seems only the metric 10 mm Petzl bolt is available. Be aware of this and have the right threads when performing your civic duty to the community.

Frank Campbell on "Crack-A-Jack." Rated a 5.9 hand-crack in 1976, this ultra-classic is now called 10b off-width. Photo: Joe Josephson.

Type of Climbing

More recently, the somewhat stronger 3/8" Hilti (or equivalent) bolt has been introduced on both sport climbs and multi-pitch routes. In fact, the Ghost is where the style of drilling with a Hilti on lead was developed in the Rockies (see History). In lieu of proper hangers, some routes on the Phantom Bluffs (up to 12a!) use two chain links attached to a 3/8" Hilti bolt. This practice is suspect at best and is not recommended. Use these pieces with caution, or better yet, replace them with proper hangers.

OTHER SOURCES OF INFORMATION

The World Wide Web (Internet)
Various individuals and climbing related organizations maintain sites on the World Wide Web that may contain updated information on new routes and access in the Ghost. Next time you're up late with nothing better to do, check out the following resources.

Rocky Mountain Books: www.rmbooks.com
Rock n' Road: www.rocknroad.com/
The Calgary Mountain Club: www.geocities.com/Yosemite/4163/
The Alpine Club of Canada: www.culturenet.ca/acc/

Calgary Mountain Club
Ghost River updates and beta of varying reliability and objectivity often appear in the "Calgary Mountain Club World News" (CMCWN)—the definitive tabloid of the Canadian Rockies scene (and any other place or person that gets in the way). For information on, copies of, or you want to send in your own drivel (don't worry, they publish everything) to this highly respected, quasi-quarterly tome write in any available format to:

CMCWN
2208 7th Ave NW
Calgary, AB T2N 0Z6
fax: (403) 264-5376
e.mail: ddornian@telusplanet.net

Remember, if you climb (or just hang out) around here long enough your name will appear in the CMCWN in a context of uncertain quality. If you respect your name and reputation you'll need to order up and stay on top of what's said and by whom (if they use their real name, that is).

A classic Ghost River climbing experience–
circa the late seventies. Photo: Albi Sole.

HAZARDS

The Road
The access road is perhaps the most legendary and maligned aspect of the Ghost River. This rough, pot-holed, washed-away, mud-filled, rock-infested endurance test is what has kept the Ghost River a relatively unvisited rock climbing venue. Many a muffler and oil pan have been sacrificed over the years. In the past, the road's reputation was far worse than it deserved. The authors have seen just about every type of vehicle in the Ghost including everything from Buicks, Westfalias, 4WDs and mobile homes to taxi cabs. More recently, however, the road has been falling into a worse state of disrepair. Check out the "Getting There" section on page 17 for more details. Good luck!

Rockfall
As per any rock climbing area, particularly on limestone, rockfall can occur at anytime. The biggest concern is climber-generated rockfall by the leader or other parties above. Helmets are highly recommended for all multi-pitch routes and many of the shorter cragging routes, particularly Borderline Buttress and Sentinel Bluff.

Naturally-occurring rockfall can also happen, sometimes on a catastrophic level. Check out the devastation below Epitaph Wall that occurred sometime in the winter of 1996. If faced with these circumstances, blame it on fate and pray for the best. The high winds common to the Ghost can also dislodge scree or blocks from ledges or the top of the crag. Clumsy mountain sheep have also been known to torment climbers with rockfall. Despite all these warnings, rockfall is the exception, not the rule.

Hazards

Ticks

The Ghost has a high resident ungulate population. Mountain sheep are abundant and moose, deer and bear are also common. As a result, spring time in the Ghost also means Rocky Mountain wood tick time. They are abundant from April (earlier if it is warm) until late June. The area around West Phantom Crag is particularly bad as it faces south and is relatively warm and dry. Ticks usually don't attach themselves right away and will be found crawling around your clothes and neck for up to several hours. It is recommended that you check all your gear and clothing closely as soon as you arrive at the car. If you still find one when you get home, flush it down the toilet, not the sink (believe it or not they'll get caught in the trap and crawl back out—they are tough little buggers). To date, the serious condition called Lyme disease, which is common elsewhere, is not known to exist in this area.

Rats

Bushy-tailed wood rats (*Neotoma cinerea*) or more affectionately known as pack rats, are common although you may never see one. The smelly, offending nests that are commonly seen on Yamnuska are strangely absent in the Ghost. However, if you leave any gear at the base or are looking for a rappel sling, expect to find tattered threads. Carry fresh rappel slings and don't leave chewable gear overnight at the crags.

Bears

The Ghost is bear country. Both black bears and grizzlies live in and frequent the area. When camping, store all food in the car overnight and while out climbing. Take precautions not to spill or pour excess food and drinks on the ground as the smell will attract bears. Dump grey water and leftovers in a firepit and burn it. Not only does it keep the bears away, but it helps preserve the fragile (and often over-used) campsites. For more information on avoiding bears, consult one of the many popular books on the subject.

Weather

Wind is the main ingredient throughout the Ghost. Even the high south-facing crags can turn icy with a stiff breeze. It is advised to carry plenty of pile layers and a wind jacket (Gore-Tex® recommended) on most days.

The Ghost seems to enjoy the same "rain shadow" effect found on Yamnuska. It may be raining (or snowing) in Banff/Canmore, but the thunderheads seem to break up as they get blown through the narrow valleys of the Ghost only to reform over Calgary. Nevertheless, the winds will be violent, the temperatures will drop, and if a storm does hit the Ghost be prepared—they are usually severe.

THE THREE R'S

Regulations

Just about the only regulations governing present climbing areas concern Banff National Park. It is illegal to camp or drive beyond the park boundary in Devil's Gap. Park wardens regularly perform border patrols and if you are caught camping or driving in the park it will result in a nasty fine and you'll give the rest of us climbers a bad name. The boundary is obviously marked by yellow pickets and a cut line. The following crags and climbs lie within Banff National Park: Planters Valley, Spectre Crag, Arrowhead, Wild West Wall, Kemp Shield, Bonanza, Grey Ghost Wall, Epitaph Wall, Spirit Pillar and Borderline Buttress. The remainder of the Ghost region is crown land where there are few or no governing regulations (except for the Ghost River Wilderness, which begins 10 km west of the North Ghost parking and far from most climbs in this book). All that is asked is that everyone show some decency and respect for the land, each other and the fragile ecosystem that makes the Ghost such a wonderful place to be.

Registration

Technically, for climbs within Banff Park you can register with the warden service. This would entail driving two hours out of the way to Banff. Plus, rescue in the Ghost is difficult at best (see below). In other words, registering is not a realistic option.

Rescue

If you require a rescue, don't expect much, if any, help. It is a one hour-long drive just to get to the nearest phone. Cell phones sometimes work from the Ghost but don't count on it. The Banff warden service is responsible for rescues within the park and Kananaskis Country personnel are responsible for all other areas. Remember this is a remote and difficult area and rescues cannot be undertaken as they might on Yamnuska or around Banff. Helicopters, medics and rescue personnel may take days to reach you if they can at all. If you get into a bind the only ones around to help you will be you and your partner(s)—so don't. For the sake of completeness here's the number:

RCMP, Cochrane (403) 932-2211.

Guides

If you want to climb in the Ghost but don't have the vehicle or the experience to go on your own, there are numerous qualified guides and schools in the Canmore region that have strong knowledge and experience of the area. Call Alpine Specialists (403) 678-3386, Larry Stanier Mountain Guide (403) 678-6628, Yamnuska Mountain School (403) 678-4164 or The Company of Canadian Mountain Guides (403) 678-3618.

Access Map

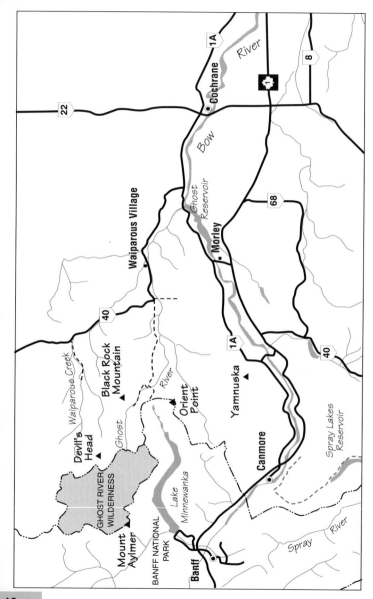

GETTING THERE

Because finding your way around the Ghost can be a taxing experience for the newcomer, access will be described in three stages. The first, "General Access" (see below), will get you from either Calgary or Banff/Canmore to the Big Hill that provides access to all the areas. Every established route can be reached from one of three main parking areas, all diverging from the Big Hill. "Parking Access" gets you from the Big Hill to your desired area and is described in the introduction to each of the main areas. The third stage, "Approach Details," will take you from your car to a specific crag. The approach details for each cliff can be found in its individual chapter.

General Access

The Ghost can be reached in 60 to 90 minutes from either Calgary or Canmore.

From Calgary, head west on Highway 1A (Crowchild Trail) to the town of Cochrane (your last chance for gas) and a four-way stop junction with Highway 22. Continue west through the stop for 13.4 km to a right (north) turn on to the Secondary Route 940 (Forestry Trunk Road), also known as Highway 40.

From Banff/Canmore, the quickest route is to follow the Trans-Canada Highway east to the Chief Chiniki/Morley turnoff and follow the Morley Road north to the 1A highway then turn right. SR 940 is another 15.5 km east (4 km past the Ghost Reservoir).

Once on the SR 940, continue northwest for about 25 km to a gated gravel road on your left about 100 m **beyond** the junction with Richard's Road. Be sure to re-close the gate if you found it that way. Just as you turn onto the gravel road, there will be a large ranch house on the hill to the right. Bear right at a fork after 3 km, just beyond a small bridge. Follow the rough, ever-worsening road for another 13.5 km to the infamous Big Hill overlooking the Ghost River Valley (running north to south) and Devil's Gap (straight ahead). At the bottom of the hill there is a sign, "Black Rock Lookout Hiking Trail." All further access descriptions with one exception (the Anti-Ghost) start from this point.

Most vehicles will be able to reach the top of the hill, and if yours isn't up to the rigours of the Ghost itself, park in a clearing on the right at the top of the hill. Devil's Gap is about a 30 minute walk from here. If you wish to climb on the more northerly crags without a vehicle, a mountain bike is recommended.

It is important to note that the Ghost River floods almost every spring. The riverbed along the base of the Big Hill is usually dry but can at times be a raging torrent. If this is the case, don't even attempt to cross by car or foot. More importantly, these floods change (i.e. eliminate) roads, carve steep banks and give the Ghost its sometimes deserved reputation for difficult access. At present (1997) it is recommended that you have good clearance or a 4WD. Faint tracks and roads abound in the Ghost. If a section ahead looks impassable, you can usually find an alternative. Take your time and if in doubt, scout ahead or walk. All parking areas are a 15-30 minute drive from the Big Hill if you don't get stuck.

CAMPING

One of the best features of the Ghost is the abundance of good, free camping, making this an ideal destination for the weekend. You can camp anywhere in the Ghost outside of Banff National Park, which prohibits any camping or overnighting. There are, however, several established campsites where most people reside. They are located as follows: 1) at the bottom of the Big Hill on the left, 2) along the park boundary in Devil's Gap, 3) next to the river near the Black Rock hiking trail, 4) at the old CMC campsite near Wully Wall, and 5) in the clearing near the start of the Bastion Wall approach. These areas are marked on the maps on pages 30 and 144. All of these areas have numerous little niches and clearings that make for fine camping.

Water
Except for the Big Hill campsite, all sites have access to water most of the summer. During spring runoff or flood, there will be water near the Big Hill. Before spring thaw and late in the season the river in Devil's Gap will dry up. To the authors' knowledge, all water in the Ghost is fit to drink as is. If you are unsure or concerned, boil or filter it.

Fire
Most well-established campsites will have fire rings, many of them outlandishly big. If you have a fire, please use an established ring. **Do not** make new fire rings or build fires directly on the ground. The ground cover in the area is very fragile. Some areas, particularly Devil's Gap, are starting to get picked clean of dead wood. **Do not cut down any trees for firewood, either live or dead-standing.** Find dead fall or better yet bring your own. During extreme fire hazards, the forest service may restrict camp fires on all crown lands. As there are no services in the Ghost, you are responsible for knowing when fires are disallowed. Call the Ghost Ranger Station at (403) 297-8800.

Human Waste
There are no outhouses in the Ghost River area. When nature calls, walk at least 200 m from any streams, climbing or camping sites and find an out of the way place, preferably in the trees. It is best to bury your waste in 6-8 inches of topsoil and burn the toilet paper. Better yet, desecrate a trash bag and carry it out with you. At the very least you should burn the paper. The most popular campsites in Devil's Gap are beginning to see white flowers (toilet paper and tampons) scattered through the trees. In general, however, waste has not been a big problem.

Please—it is up to us to keep it that way.

Top: The view from the top of Phantom Tower.
Trevor Jones and Orient Point looking south.
Bottom: The last mountain between here and Labrador. Black Rock Mountain to the northeast. Photos: Joe Josephson.

CAMPING

Garbage

Put only combustible material into a camp fire. This **does not** include plastic, tin foil, tin cans or batteries. If you do burn tins to rid of food odours, clean them out in the morning and pack them out with the rest of your garbage. Hey—this is car camping, there are absolutely no excuses. By keeping our impact minimal and our profile low, we can do our part to help maintain the unrestricted access we now enjoy, but more importantly we can endeavour to preserve the fragile ground cover and ecosystem of the Ghost. Besides, none of us really want to find a pigsty when we go camping.

SEASON

The climbing season runs from early-May to mid-October, give or take a few weeks on either end. West Phantom Crag, Phantom Bluffs and Silver-Tongued Devil Crag will have the longest season owing to their southern aspects. Because of the generally low snowpack and high winds, the rock dries out very quickly and rarely seeps. The defining features in the spring will be when the snowdrifts in the road melt away and the river is passable—see General Access on page 17. In the fall it is common to climb into late October or even November depending upon air and wind temperatures. During the winter (sometimes in mid-October) the Ghost offers an abundance of fine waterfall ice climbing. See Joe Josephson's *Waterfall Ice Climbs in the Canadian Rockies.*

LIMITATIONS OF THIS BOOK

This book is intended for the experienced climber only. It is not a manual of instruction, but a rough, if not incomplete, guide to the routes. It assumes that the reader is already proficient in the use of climbing techniques, hardware and protection, the use of a rope, and has climbed before on natural rock in the out-of-doors. Whereas this book contains much useful information, it does not take the place of skill and good judgment. Every word in this book is the subjective opinion of the authors and is not guaranteed to be 100% accurate. You, the readers, are responsible for, but not limited to, the following factors: your own safety and health, your ability to find the start of and the climbing route on any climb, your ability to judge the difficulty of the climb or any individual move on any piece of rock you may encounter, your ability to safely climb any piece of rock you say you are going to climb, your ability to descend or back off any cliff you find yourself on, your own decisions in life and climbing and, your ability to have fun.

HISTORY

Despite the limited number of established climbs, the Ghost has always enjoyed being near or at the forefront of local style. In the 25 plus years of recorded history, numerous styles and ethics have reared their head and left a stamp on Ghost River rock. These run the gamut from traditional ground-up ascents, to pre-inspected sport climbs, evolving into multi-pitch rappel bolting, to on-lead, on-sight bolting.

Rock climbing began in the area in the late sixties when members of the newly formed Calgary Mountain Club (CMC) held a series of club camps in the Minnewanka Valley. This early exploration was not documented and old pitons found later remained a mystery for many years. Some information was unearthed recently during an interview with Don Vockeroth, one of the most prolific Rockies climbers of the 1960s. Climbs had been done mainly on the lower cliffs (now called Phantom Bluffs) but according to Don, no records were kept because "any climb with less than five pitches was considered to be practice." It is likely that the pitons found on "Bandidos" and "The Grooves" on Phantom Bluffs and on the Spirit Pillar date from this period. Other members of this early group included Lloyd MacKay, Bernie Schiesser, Gunti Prinz, Deiter Raubach and Klaus Hahn.

Chris Perry

The first major climb, also unrecorded and a mystery for many years, was the "Texas Peapod" by Don Vockeroth together with P. Robbins in 1971. Nothing else happened until 1975 when the area was rediscovered by a new generation of CMCers who were unaware of the earlier exploration. Acting on a tip from that venerable source of new route potential, Urs Kallen, Chris Perry and Trevor Jones drove in for a look. From the top of the Big Hill, the sight of the Minnewanka Valley with its steep and, in some cases, overhanging walls, seemed like a promised land—a "limestone Yosemite." They were particularly struck by a large face directly above the old RCMP cabin in Devil's Gap (now burnt down), which had an appealing crack line curving up its centre. The face was reminiscent of the Dolomites where both of them had recently climbed. Not wasting any time, the pair returned the following weekend with Andy Dunlop and Martyn White to climb the now classic South Face of Phantom Tower. Once on top of the tower, with rain turning to sleet and approaching darkness a problem arose they they hadn't counted on—how to descend the huge cliff bands that extended in both directions without an apparent break. Eventually the South Phantom Crag Descent Gully was found with just enough light to reach the base of the cliffs.

For the next few years development proceeded at a rapid rate. The overall quality of the rock was significantly better than in the Bow Valley and there were numerous crack and corner lines that offered good natural gear and piton protection. The mostly expatriated British climbers considered bolts unethical and this limited the scope of development. Jack Firth and Canadian, Pat Morrow, joined Chris and

History

Trevor to produce seven multi-pitch climbs by the end of 1975. A report by Chris Perry in the Canadian Alpine Journal summed up the enthusiasm at the time. The term "Limestone Yosemite" was used and the article ended with a tongue-in-cheek quote, that "In a few years time when Calgary climbers talk of going to the 'Valley' they'll mean the Ghost River Valley."

Jack Firth

Regular CMC camps-cum-parties took place and the number of devotees increased as did the quality of the climbs. Prominent additions were Bugs McKeith, Jeff Upton, Albi Sole and perhaps most of all Nigel Hellewell. Access was even more difficult than today so the action centred close to the CMC campsite on North Phantom Crag and Wully Wall. But when "Bonanza" was climbed in early 1976 with its exciting descent by a single rappel, this helped open up the spectacular south-facing cliffs above Devil's Gap. "Grey Ghost" was climbed by Trevor Jones and Jack Firth and the well-known British climber Pat Littlejohn added "Banshee" along with local Ian Staples. The 1976 season culminated in North Phantom Crag's superb "Crack-A-Jack" (5.10b) by Jack Firth and Jeff Horne. This came closest to their ideal of a "limestone Yosemite."

The pace continued during the 1977 season with a collection of outstanding new climbs. The moderate "Consolation," added by Chris Perry and Martyn White, boasts excellent rock and an outstanding position and has remained one of the most travelled routes in the region. Many of the others like "The Wraith," "Thor," and "Satan" were largely the work of Nigel Hellewell. "Thor" follows a coveted three pitch corner on Bastion Wall. Most of the first pitch had been climbed by Chris Perry and Mike Sawyer, but before the duo could return, they were scooped midweek by Nigel and Jeff Upton. Depending upon who you talk to, "Thor" is anywhere from solid 5.10a to 5.10c and is considered the classic hard route of the seventies era. The few bolts now on the route were added on subsequent ascents.

Nigel Hellewell

History

It is important to note that "Thor" and the earlier "Crack-A-Jack" were all originally graded 5.9 because that was believed to be the max of their abilities. It was a bad habit that continues to cough up sandbags. Nigel was the first to break free and delivered the 5.10 grade with his rarely repeated "Satan" (5.10b) on Bastion Wall. This was perhaps the first route in the Rockies to deliberately be given such a distinction.

The following season would prove to be a watershed in Ghost River climbing. Wully Wall and Sentinel Crag were the favoured venues although a few obvious lines were mopped up on Phantom Tower, North Phantom Crag and Bastion Wall. Chris Perry and Nigel Hellewell continued to lead the fray with a number of challenging routes on Wully Wall in the so-called 5.8-5.9 range.

Albi Sole

Another "old style 5.9" called "Big Willy" was added by Bugs McKeith and Alan Burgess and may still be unrepeated. Meanwhile, Albi Sole and Greg Spohr polished off the obvious "Cyclops" (5.10b) on Sentinel Crag, only the second declared 5.10 in the valley. Not only were the 1978 climbs among the hardest in the Ghost, they would prove to be the last major routes of the seventies.

Andy Genereux

In 1980, Chris Perry produced the first Ghost River guidebook, which included some 40 climbs. It was hoped that the book would help continue the development and encourage others to visit the area. Instead, it marked the end of an era. How could they have seen that the eighties would usher in a revolution that would change the landscape of climbing around the world?

In 1981 the area was visited by Jeff Marshall, a young, somewhat controversial Calgary climber (Jeff drilled the Rockies first rappel-placed bolt at Wasootch in 1982) who would later do many significant firsts in the Bow Valley. En route to Phantom Tower he stopped at The Haystack and climbed the original, run-out version of "Teenage Wasteland" (5.9 R), the first recorded climb on the lower bluffs. Jeff also has a penchant for spectacular falls and on an early attempt to repeat "Thor" he fell 25 metres on the second pitch managing to break

History

Al Pickel's knee at the belay. Jeff later climbed "Thor," but he lost the second ascent (also without bolts) to another young Calgarian, Andy Genereux, along with Bill Rennie. Andy would begin to figure very prominently in and eventually dominate Ghost River climbing.

Despite these movements, only a handful of new climbs were done in the first few years following the guidebook. The focus remained on traditional styles and bolts were reluctantly used, if at all, even on the short routes. However, in 1983 climbers began to launch out of the cracks and corners and on to the sweeping, less-obvious expanses of compact grey rock. Naturally, the Grey Ghost Wall was the prime location and "Ziggurat" (5.10a) was climbed by Chris Perry and Chris Dale in September. The following month Chas Yonge, along with John Rollins, found "Mantissa" (5.9) also on the Grey Ghost Wall. These routes, how-

Chas Yonge

ever, remained dictated by the availability of natural protection and began the next era of development, which could be described as the "runout years." Prominent players were Dave Morgan, Andy Genereux, Andy Skuce and Jon Jones, although others had their moments of being "out there." Bolts were used only sparingly and placed on lead but the focus had switched from the big cliffs to the shorter, more accessible cragging areas around Phantom Bluffs and Sentinel Bluffs. Some of the notable, if not exciting, routes from this period were: "Revelations" (5.10a), "On the Border" (5.10b), "Achilles" (5.10b) and "Imbroglio" (5.10d) at

Jon Jones   Dave Morgan

Phantom Bluffs, and "Softly, Softly" (5.10b), "Prickly Fear" (5.11b) and "Last Mango in Paradise" (5.10c) all at Sentinel Bluffs. Some of these routes have since been retrofitted with new and/or more bolts.

It was Morgan who first brought the 5.11 grade to the Ghost with the ultra-classic "Alberta Jam" in 1982. This challenging offset crack remains the hardperson's plum and although it is only 5.11b/c it has yet to receive an onsight ascent. The years 1983 through 1985 saw an important change in local values that eventually led the way to the modern sport climbs of the present era. The main Ghost activists in this new pur-

History

Frank Campbell

suit were Andy Genereux and Jon Jones who found one pitch routes that were cleaned and bolted on rappel. But in these early days of this new ethic top roping was rarely employed and runouts were intentionally created to simulate on-sight placements with certain amounts of boldness built in. Prime examples of this early but short-lived ethical style are "The Chimera" (5.10c R) and "Rhydd" (5.10b), both at Borderline Buttress. It has only been through the adamant insistence of Genereux that "The Chimera" has to this day retained its original character as most others have since been retrofitted.

Beginning around 1985, true sport climbing tactics began to take hold in the Canadian Rockies. The Ghost was no exception and the movement was toward closely-placed bolts, pre-inspection and top roping. A small group of activists were in charge of the majority of the new routes. They consisted of Dave Morgan, Jon Jones, Chas Yonge, Andy Skuce and Andy Genereux.

Morgan was quickly joined by Genereux to firmly establish the 5.11 grade with a variety of classic sport routes like "Cryin' Mercy" (5.11b), "Edge Clinger (5.11b) and "Boy Wonder" (5.11c). These routes culminated in the spectacular arching dihedral "Sunset Boulevard" (5.11c/d) and the region's first 5.12, "Superwoman's Wildest Dream" by Genereux in 1989.

During the mid-eighties the Ghost became a Mecca for waterfall ice climbing. The undisputed leader of this movement was Frank Campbell. During that same period Frank began to look at the untapped traditional-style rock climbs. Along with Paul Stoliker and several other friends, they developed three completely new areas: Planters Valley, Spectre Crag and Silver-Tongued Devil Crag along with numerous climbs in the Waiparous Creek drainage. Many of these routes cleaned up on classic, obvious lines and filled a much needed void for quality, moderate climbs.

The breakthrough, multi-pitch route of the mid-eighties was found on Epitaph Wall. The prominent right-leaning grey streak was for years considered the best line in the Ghost. However, the early activists didn't use bolts and thus didn't con-

Trevor Jones

History

sider climbing the route's immaculate yet compact rock. In 1987, "Creamed Cheese" (5.11a) finally fell to the determined efforts of Brian Gross and Choc Quinn with the minimal use of bolts (not for the faint at heart). This monumental route has bold runouts on 5.10 terrain and is generally considered the most classic and sought after route in the Ghost.

The dawning of the nineties saw a continued development of sport climbs in the established areas as well as the incredible Kemp Shield. But it was Andy Genereux's multi-pitch "Dirty Dancing" (5.11d/12a) that was the most outstanding addition in 1991. With four back-to-back 5.11 pitches and a recent optional 5.11-5.12 approach pitch, it remains unrepeated. The climb was started traditionally on lead, but owing to a crack filled with mud, this method was abandoned in lieu of rappel bolting and cleaning. Because of overgrown cracks and short sections of loose rock, this may prove to be the first ascent style of choice for several of the steep faces in the area. Nevertheless, "Dirty Dancing" is one of only two multi-pitch routes yet completed from the top down.

Joe Josephson

One of the most consistent activists over the years has been original Ghost veteran Trevor Jones. In 1990, he and Blob Wyvill extended the now up-graded "Crack-A-Jack" to the top of North Phantom Crag with four excellent pitches of "The Separate Reality" (5.10b/c). Later in 1992, along with Joe Josephson, Trevor added major variations to the long-lost routes "The Wraith" (5.9) and "South Face of Phantom Tower" (5.9), as well as establishing numerous cragging routes in the Spirit Pillar and Phantom Cracks area.

Inspired by Trevor, JoJo continued to unearth some notable-but-forgotten gems at Sentinel and Silver-Tongued Devil crags and added his own "Tough Trip Through Paradise" (5.10b) with Bruce Hendricks in 1993. This was the first ascent of the heretofore unclimbed South Phantom Crags.

Soon after the first ascent of "Dirty Dancing," a new style appeared; one that has created some of the finest multi-pitch climbs in the Rockies. The style is ground-up, bolting on-lead with a power (Hilti) gun. In 1993, Genereux and Tim Pochay opened the gates with their instant classic "Southern Exposure" (5.11a) on Grey Ghost Wall. Genereux was the driving force behind "Windmills of the Mind" (drilled on-lead without hooks at 5.11b), "Zephyr" (5.10d) and "Wully Sport" (5.11b/c). This latter route includes one of the harder crack pitches on local limestone. Although all of these routes require natural gear, they are predominantly protected and belayed from bolts. By using the drill, climbers have been able to stray away from the natural cracks and corners that generally hold the loosest rock, and by climbing them from the ground up, these routes preserve a large adventure component.

In pure Ghost tradition, however, older values have continued to ring true with the addition of "Prosopopoeia" (5.11b/c) on Epitaph Wall in 1995 by Keith Haberl and Shep Steiner. Climbed between bitter August storms in a one-day effort, the

History

pair used only one bolt on this committing route that finished up "Creamed Cheese" in the pouring rain and darkness. It is easily the hardest, traditional, multi-pitch route in the Ghost.

Sport climbing has continued to inch along, although only small selections of the potential have been touched. The primary venues have been Wild West Wall and Spirit Pillar. The former has, to date, produced the finest sport climbs in the Ghost, highlighted by Pochay and Genereux's mega-classics "Blade Runner" (5.12a) and the spectacular "Dreams of Verdon" (5.11c). This latter six-pitch route was completed in 1996 from the top down after several efforts over three years. With five pitches going at mid-5.11, "Dreams of Verdon" is the hallmark sport climb of the Ghost.

Tim Pochay

As late as the early nineties you could characterize climbing activity in the Ghost as follows: 95% of all people rock climbing in the Ghost did the classic "Bonanza" and that route might have seen five ascents a year. That didn't add up to a whole lot of climbers. Slowly that has begun to change. "Thor," "Southern Exposure," "The Wraith" and even "Creamed Cheese" have begun to see enough ascents that we can't keep track of them all. This book coincides with a golden age of Ghost River rock climbing.

Today there are over 200 routes (almost 100 multi-pitch) established in this wonderful area. The surface has hardly been scratched and the potential barely explored. Classic climbs await those with a spirit of adventure and who still want a challenge in their climbing experience.

Some people think this book will ruin the Ghost. Indeed, this volume will likely increase traffic. But if we all adhere to a standard of decency and respect, the Ghost will remain a perfect place to camp, to seek adventure and to enjoy the experience of climbing in one of the Rockies truly special places. Together the authors have almost 50 years of experience in the area. Our reasoning behind this book is to share the wonders of the area and inspire others to experience and treat the Ghost with the same admiration and respect we have given it.

Andy Dunlop, Trevor Jones and Martyn White on an early CMC trip in 1975, resulting in the first ascent of Phantom Tower. Photo Chris Perry.

USING THIS GUIDE

The climbing areas will be described in a clockwise sequence starting with the southern crags and moving north. The climbs on each cliff (except for noted exceptions) will be described in a left to right fashion. Unless indicated, all directions for approach, while climbing, and for rappelling will assume that the climbers are facing the rock. For downclimbing, directions assume that climbers are facing out.

The Parking Access and Approach Details in each chapter take you from the standard parking area to the base of the cliff only. To find your way to the Ghost, please refer to the "Getting There" section on page 17.

When available, we have included topos. It is important to note that because a route does not have a topo it doesn't mean that it's not worth doing. The reason for no topo is probably because the authors could not get adequate information. New topos and updates to existing ones are greatly appreciated.

A star system is used to indicate route quality. All stars refer to and are compared to climbs in the Ghost River only. No comparison or illusion toward other climbs or areas is intended. If a climb does not have a star rating it does not imply that the climb is not worth doing. It simply means that there may not have been enough information or a consensus to arrive at a star rating. If we know a route to be truly poor, we will tell you.

Consider the following story. In 1992, two Calgary climbers went to climb the then obscure route "The Wraith." After two attempts (one thwarted by a rainstorm) they finished the route (a possible second ascent) to find what is perhaps the most sustained and best 5.9 route in the area including Yamnuska (it was originally graded 5.8). The moral of the story is this: the Ghost has a reputation for coughing up forgotten gems (another one was "Duveinafees," rediscovered in 1996). One reason many of the older routes don't have stars is because not much is known about them. If you happen to find a forgotten gem, do a new route, or have corrected information on any established route, please contact the authors at the following address:

Rocky Mountain Books
#4 Spruce Centre SW
Calgary, AB
T3C 3B3
email: jojo@telusplanet.net

Ben Firth on-sighting "Blade Runner."
Photo: Paul Valiulis.

Devil's Gap

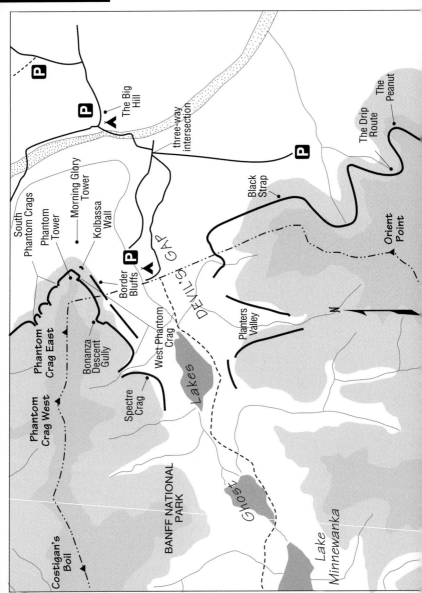

ORIENT POINT

Orient Point is the most easterly of the peaks on the south side of the Minnewanka Valley. See the map on page 30. It is a massive and complex mountain, surrounded almost entirely by cliff bands. Aside from the climbs in Planters Valley, however, only three rock climbs have been established. Each climb is unique, if not bizarre. They stand testimony to the exploration of Ghost pioneer Frank Campbell. The three climbs are described below and those in Planters Valley are covered in the Devil's Gap section starting on page 35.

"The Peanut" is an intriguing pinnacle located in a notch between a much larger outlying pinnacle and the east ridge of Orient Point. It is only distinguishable as a separate feature when viewed from near the three-way intersection at the entrance to the Minnewanka Valley. From here, it is located approximately due south. It has a long approach and is perhaps a climb to do just "because it is there."

"The Drip" was done to serve as an approach to "The Big Drip," a waterfall ice climb that forms in one of the large bowls on the east side of Orient Point, north of "The Peanut." This huge curtain of ice rarely extends down past a halfway ledge and is usually reached via a lengthy approach from above. This three pitch rock route was established to access the ice from below on warm and sunny winter days.

The remaining climb, "Black Strap," was completed for more conventional reasons— it climbs an interesting feature on generally good rock. It is currently the only climb on a large band of cliffs that angles slightly up and left across the east side of the northern subsidiary peak of Orient Point. The cliffs face the access road directly when viewed from between the Big Hill and the three-way intersection and are situated immediately below the summit of the subsidiary peak. A huge open corner at the apex of a large scree cone breaks through the cliff band just left of centre, and immediately left of this is a buttress with a rounded nose of rock on its left side that extends almost to the top. A shallow, right-facing corner system forms the right side of the nose, and at the top of this on the right is a prominent, square-cut overhang. This overhang, and one on the opposite side, form two "eyes" above the "nose." "Black Strap" climbs the corner to the top of the nose and continues up to the top of the cliff. Despite its relatively long approach, it is reported to be a worthwhile route.

The extensive cliff bands on Orient Point have received little attention because many of them face north and east and are relatively difficult to access. The area around "Black Strap" and the waterworn walls above the ice climb "Wicked Wanda" appear to be the most promising areas for new climbs.

Approach Details
Approach for the first two climbs is described from the three-way intersection mentioned in the Devil's Gap parking access, see page 36.

A. The Peanut
B. The Drip
C. Black Strap, see opposite

The Peanut 15 m, 5.7

F. Campbell & O. Miskiw, June 1987

This climb definitely has the worst ratio of good climbing to approach length than any other in the guidebook. However, the appeal of this little pinnacle, tucked in a distant notch, is undeniable. If no one else will go, ask Frank, he is probably good for the second ascent!

From the three-way intersection, head due south on the River Road and park as close as possible to the gully on the north side of the notch. Take the line of least resistance up through the trees and then climb the gully (4th class) to the notch. Climb the wall on the left (east) side of the pinnacle to a piton belay at the top.

Descend by rappel.

The larger outlying pinnacle can also be climbed at easy 5th class.

The Drip 95 m, 5.8+

F. Campbell & P. Stoliker, 1986

This route lies in the left hand of two major bowls, readily seen from the top of the Big Hill, on the east face of Orient Point. At the three-way intersection, head south on the River Road for almost 2 km to a small drainage that comes down from the two bowls. Hike directly up the drainage and at a Y-junction, follow the left fork up into a bowl below the waterfall. Scramble up to the top of the scree/snow cone on the right of the waterfall and begin slightly to the right.

1. 40 m, 5.8. Climb up for a few metres and then traverse left to a large flake. Either squeeze up the more secure, inside chimney or go up the outside of the flake to the top. Continue up a left-facing corner to a piton belay.

Orient Point

2. 10 m, 5.5. Move right across a ledge to a fixed rappel station by a right-facing corner.
3. 45 m, 5.8+. Climb up and right to a bolt and then go back left to some small flakes. Move up to a piton and continue past two bolts (5.8+) to a groove on the left. Go up this to a fixed station on a big ledge. This ledge leads left to the waterfall.

Descend the route in two full rappels.

Black Strap

Orient Point

*Black Strap 200 m, 5.8
J. Rowe & F. Campbell, May 1984

This interesting climb has had several ascents. However, the description given below was "interpreted" from two slightly contradictory sources. As such, pitch lengths are approximate so do the climb expecting a grading sandbag.

The approach is reportedly not as bad as it looks. Start at the park boundary as for other climbs in Devil's Gap (see page 36). Walk south directly up the cut line marking the boundary to a large cairn at the top of a hill. Continue south for about 50 m to an east-west horse trail that goes along the bench a few hundred metres above the valley floor. Follow the horse trail to a point below and slightly right of the large scree cone noted on page 30. Walk up through fairly open trees and continue up the right side of the scree cone to some house-sized blocks near the top. Move over to the left side and then scramble up and left (3rd class) following ledges past the outside of some small pinnacles (ignore an obvious gully on the right). Move up and left over a short step to the end of easy ground, below and about 6 m right of a right-facing corner. The main upper corner on the right side of the "nose" is now some distance up and to the left, out of view.

1. 45 m, 5.8. Move up and traverse left into the corner. Climb the wide crack in the corner to below a loose-looking section (#11 Hex), and then traverse left on to the edge and go up to a small belay.
2. 40 m, 5.6. Easy climbing leads up and left into the main corner system.
3. 45 m, 5.8. Climb the crack in the corner to a steep section and then move out left to belay.
4. 30 m, 5.7. The next pitch climbs the left wall of the corner to the top of the "nose." Go up left across the wall and then back right for a short distance to a see-through crack. Climb the crack and continue up past loose blocks to a good crack that leads to easy ground and the top of the "nose." Move right to a fixed belay and rappel station immediately left of the large roof.
5. 40 m, 5.7. Make a short, loose traverse left and then go up to a block at the base of a crack. Climb the crack to a tree belay at the top of the cliff.

To descend, move across right (north) to a good tree with a small cairn above and rappel past a large overhang to the fixed station at the top of pitch 4 (45 m). The second rappel leads to a ledge system (45 m) on the right wall of the corner; walk north along this to the next station (bolt and piton). Continue down past a third fixed station at a ledge (40 m) to easy scrambling at the base of the cliff (30 m).

DEVIL'S GAP

Devil's Gap or the Lake Minnewanka Valley is the premier rock climbing venue in the Ghost River. This is owing mostly to the southern exposure of the cliffs on the north side of the Gap. These are also the most consistently high cliffs around with perhaps the greatest potential for more quality routes. Of the eight major walls on the north side, each one reaches at least 200 metres in height with several striving for well over 300 metres.

The four easternmost formations are spurs off the Phantom Crag massif and are the only formations with recorded climbs. Each are separated by gullies of varying size and character. They are from east to west: 1) Phantom Tower, 2) Epitaph Wall and Grey Ghost Wall, 3) Bonanza Wall and Wild West Wall and 4) Spectre Crag. The Epitaph, Grey Ghost, Bonanza and Wild West walls are known collectively as West Phantom Crag.

Spectre Crag is the most-westerly of any developed venue. The large wall that is the continuation of Spectre Crag to the left remains untapped. Perhaps the most intriguing formations beyond here are the two massive caves that form the bottom of a 330 m cliff (perhaps the highest in Devil's Gap) just above the second Ghost Lake. These are near the waterfall routes "Dr. Heckle" and "Mr. Jive." With a mountain bike, they can be reached in about 45 minutes from the park boundary.

On the south side of Devil's Gap, we have considerably less to say. Most of the walls face due north and with the high winds common to the Ghost they are likely to be rather cold. However, this side of the valley does hold numerous cliffs on several levels as well as one of the most consistently overhanging sections in the entire Ghost. This spectacular cliff looms over Lake Minnewanka and appears to overhang 150 metres out of 200+!

Yet aside from Planters Valley on the west side of Orient Point there are no other established routes on the south side of Devil's Gap proper.

Devil's Gap

Parking Access

Devil's Gap, also known as the Minnewanka Valley, gives access to the following crags: Orient Point, Planters Valley, Spectre Crag, West Phantom Crag (which includes Arrowhead, Wild West Wall, Kemp Shield, Bonanza, Grey Ghost Wall, Epitaph Wall and Spirit Pillar), Phantom Tower and the various Phantom Bluffs.

At the Black Rock Lookout sign at the bottom of the Big Hill, turn left and go a short distance to a steep break in the bank that puts you into the riverbed. Follow various cobblestone roads south until it is possible to cross near the south end of a large artificial (rocks and chain link) embankment. Beware of another steep bank climbing out of the river. Follow a good road south for about 100 m to where it turns west. Shortly after the road turns west there is a three-way intersection. At this point the Banff Park service has attempted to erect a sign indicating the approaching park boundary and some previously published descriptions for the area include this sign. However, the sign rarely lasts more than a few weeks before one of the many maraudin' offroadin' recreationists takes care of it. Anyway....

The first branch, referred to as the "River Road," turns due south (left) and leads along the east side of Orient Point for an indeterminate distance. The remaining two offshoots both lead into Devil's Gap.

The middle branch turns left, goes down a bank, across the flats, then winds through the trees for another 2 km to a large sign indicating Banff Park. Make a sharp right turn and go a short distance to a meadow near the river. Park here—it is illegal to drive farther and it doesn't get you closer to the climbs anyway.

If you go straight from the three-way intersection the road picks its way across gravel flats and through trees past a variety of parking/camping areas. Follow a good gravel track along a large diversion bank to a break on the left that gives access to the above-mentioned meadow area near the park boundary.

Access via the middle branch is dictated by ruts that are sometimes deep and muddy. A short wheelbase or high clearance is recommended for this option. Be careful in the spring when the road is muddy or drifted with snow. The straight-ahead variation is tough if you're short on power/traction and you might get bogged down in loose cobblestones and gravel. If either of these sounds iffy—walk.

PLANTERS VALLEY

Planters Valley is the only major climbing area, to date, on the south side of the Minnewanka Valley. The quality of the rock on established climbs is well above average and only a few of the routes have been repeated—beware of grading sandbags. The area is characterized by predominately crack climbing and a small selection of pitons is recommended for all routes. The climbs are located on cliffs along both the east and west sides of the valley. They are all before (north of) a narrow canyon that leads through to the upper drainage and the "Peanut Gallery" ice climbs. The cliffs are referred to as East and West Planters walls.

Approach

From the large sign at the park boundary, follow the Lake Minnewanka trail west, crisscrossing a rough track known as the Gravel Trough Road for the first kilometre or so. Stay on the main trail on the south side of the valley until directly below the Planters Valley drainage (15-20 minutes). Cut up through open, treed slopes to gain the creekbed and then follow it up to the climbing areas. There is usually some water seeping through the rocks in the lower part of the valley although it may dry up in hot weather. All the routes require about an hour approach from the car.

West Planters Wall

A. South End
B. Nutcracker Sweet

West Planters Wall

This varied cliff lies on the right side of the valley and is slightly shorter than its opposing neighbour. Although it is one cliff, the three areas with established routes are noticeably distinct and separated. See photos on pages 37 and 39. They are described from north to south as you will encounter them. The entire area gets the sun first thing and is in the shade by late morning or early afternoon. Be forewarned, even on the hottest days the belays can get cool if a wind is blowing.

*The Scar 150 m, 5.9
J. A. Owen & F. Campbell, June 1987

At the north end of West Planters Valley Wall there is an area of grey slabby rock bounded on the left by a corner and a steep yellow wall. Immediately left of the yellow wall there is a striking, right-slanting corner system, capped by a large roof. "The Scar" climbs the corner system and exits to the right around the roof.

Approach
Walk up Planters Valley to a large scree gully directly below the climb. Continue up the creek for a short distance to a large talus slope, ascend through trees right of the talus, and then follow a ridge between the talus slope and the scree gully to reach the main cliff just left of a lower cliff band. Traverse right along ledges above the lower cliffs and then go up to an alcove at the base of the main corner. The first pitch climbs a short buttress on the left side of the alcove to gain the main corner system above.

1. 25 m, 5.7. Beginning just left of the main corner line, climb the wall to a right-facing corner and follow it to a belay ledge by a block on the left.
2. 30 m, 5.5. Traverse right and down slightly to gain the main corner system and climb up easily to a good ledge on the right side where the wall steepens (bolt).
3. 5.9. Climb up and right to a steep face and continue up past a bolt to an overhang. Move left and go over the overhang (5.9), then continue up toward a vertical crack. Belay on the right (bolt).
4. 5.8. Continue up past a bolt on the right wall and then follow the corner to a stance on the right below the large roof.
5. 20 m, 5.6. Climb up and right below the roof and then go up to a tree belay at the top.

Descend by rappelling from trees at the north end of the cliff, just beyond the section of grey slabby rock. Careful choice of tree location and two 50 m ropes is required.

The Scar

West Planters Wall

The Nutcracker Sweet (sic)

Approximately at the centre of West Planters Valley Wall there is a huge right-facing corner, and immediately to its right is an area of extremely solid, black rock set at an average angle of about 70 degrees. "Acorn-er" follows the right-facing corner, and three climbs, known collectively as the "Nutcracker Sweet," climb the slabby section on the right. All four climbs end at a fault line that marks the top of the good rock although an unrecommended exit has been climbed (5.9).

Approach

Continue up the creekbed past "The Scar" to a scree slope directly below the climbs. Hike up through open glades on the right-hand margin of the scree to reach the climbs. At the bottom of the "Nutcracker Sweet" area there is a prominent scree cone and all climbs are located relative to this.

Descent

The four climbs share a common rappel descent down the route "Nutcracker Sweet: First Movement." There are two 50 m rappels from chained anchors. Refer to the "First Movement" route description for their locations.

*Acorn-er 120 m, 5.9

P. Stoliker, L. DeMarsh & M. Haden, Oct. 1987

The climbing in the upper corner is interesting and well protected. Start about 50 m below and left of the scree cone at three small trees, below and slightly to the right of the main corner.

1. 40 m, 5.3. Follow a blocky corner up and left to the first awkward section.
2. 45 m, 5.6. Continue up the corner for about 7 m to easy ground. Move up and right and then climb yellow rock on the left to a ledge about 10 m below a huge roof.
3. 35 m, 5.9. Move up and right to a ledge. Avoid the next ugly-looking section of the corner by moving right on the ledge and then climbing a groove back left. Follow the obvious jam-crack up and around a roof to the fault line.
4. 40 m, 4th. Traverse right along the fault line to the Nutcracker Sweet descent.

*Nutcracker Sweet: First Movement 115 m, 5.8

P. Stoliker & L. DeMarsh, Aug. 1987

Despite mostly excellent rock the climb is, in places, difficult to protect without pitons; most noticeably on the first pitch and the final corner. Start about 5 m right (north) of the apex of the scree cone.

1. 35 m, 5.7. Climb up to a scree ledge. Follow steps up and left to another scree ledge. Move up and left along the ledge to an alcove (piton—hidden at the back of small edge), about 7 m below and slightly left of a large corner crack (Second Movement).
2. 40 m, 5.7. Step left from the belay and move up for about 4 m to the bottom of a finger crack. This crack is 3 m left of the large crack on the "Second Movement."

West Planters Wall

Make a few moves up the finger crack then take a difficult step left to easier ground in a corner. Go up to a large ledge with a rappel chain. Move left along the ledge and follow an obvious corner to a small ledge at the bottom of a crack (small-med friends useful for the belay).

3. 40 m, 5.8. Climb the crack to a loose block. Climb up right on big holds then step left over the block to a large ledge, being careful not to disturb the block. From the left side of the ledge, climb a slanting corner to a ledge. Step up to a piton and continue right to an open book with a tiny crack. Stem the open book (crux—knifeblade recommended) to the fault line and step right to a bolt/piton belay with chains.

**Nutcracker Sweet: Second Movement 100 m, 5.8

P. Stoliker & L. DeMarsh, Sept. 1987

This climb starts just left of "First Movement" and crosses it at the first belay and then again just before the fault line.

1. 25 m, 5.8. Climb the steep left-trending crack about 5 m left of the apex of the scree cone and then continue up and right over easy steps to belay as for "First Movement" (piton).

2. 45 m, 5.8. Climb the wide crack above and slightly right of the belay, then continue up easier cracks to a ledge at the bottom of an inside corner with a large crack 3 m to its left. Climb the corner and then step left to the base of another corner at the top of the wide crack. Move up to a good belay in an alcove a few metres higher.

3. 30 m, 5.8. Climb straight up for 3 m and then left for 7 m to join "First Movement." Follow "First Movement" for a short distance to the open book about 7 m below the fault line. The original line moves left for 2 m, then up and left over a slab (often wet) to the fault line. It is recommended, however, to finish straight up the corner as per the "First Movement."

*Nutcracker Sweet: Third Movement 95 m, 5.8

P. Stoliker, L. DeMarsh & M. Haden, Oct. 1987

Start about 20 m left of the top of the scree cone and scramble up and left to the bottom of two cracks.

1. 40 m, 5.7. Climb the steep right-hand crack past loose-looking blocks for about 4 m to a ledge. Move up and right over easy ground to the base of a large crack in a left-facing corner. Follow the corner to a ledge below a finger crack.

2. 45 m, 5.8. Climb the crack to a ledge and then follow "First Movement" up to the fault line.

West Planters Wall South End

The first three climbs are located immediately to the right (north) of a broken, stepped buttress that extends almost down to the creekbed just before the canyon. This section of the cliff is referred to as the "South End" of West Planters Wall.

The best route at the South End starts by climbing "Nuts and Bolts" to where it crosses "Wall Nut" and then follows that route to the top. This gives a fine, sustained, three-pitch climb (5.8, 5.10b, 5.10a **).

Approach
Scramble up scree slopes immediately north of the buttress to reach the main cliff near "Peanut Dogleg," a prominent right-facing open book leading up to stepped overhangs that trend up to the right.

Descent
All three climbs descend the buttress, by two 50 m rappels from trees.

*Peanut Dogleg 95 m, 5.8
P. Stoliker & J. A. Owen, June 1987

"Peanut Dogleg" follows the obvious corner/roof line noted above.
1. 45 m, 5.8. Climb the open book to a good belay ledge about 10 m below a roof.
2. 50 m, 5.8. Continue up the corner and then follow the roof line right to finish up a narrow chimney. Easy climbing leads to trees at the top.

Nuts and Bolts 130 m, 5.10b
P. Stoliker & S. Brucke, July 1988

This route starts left of "Wall Nut," crosses it at half height and then finishes on mediocre rock up and to the right. Start 10 m left of "Wall Nut" at a right-facing corner.
1. 35 m, 5.8. Climb the corner for about 7 m to a ledge. Move up and left past a piton and then traverse right to a bolt and wired nut. Climb up past a second bolt to a 2-bolt belay just below a left-facing corner.
2. 30 m, 5.10b. Move up with difficulty past a bolt to a crack in the corner and follow this to the ledge on pitch 2 of "Wall Nut" (piton). Traverse easily right and down to the piton belay in an alcove at the top of the first pitch of that route.
3. 40 m, 5.7. Move up and right over easy but loose rock, and then go back up and left on better rock to a tree.
4. 25 m, 5.6. Climb a corner to the top.

West Planters Wall South End

A. Peanut Dogleg
B. Nuts & Bolts
C. Wall Nut
○ Rappel points

44

West Planters Wall South End

*Wall Nut 115 m, 5.10a
P. Stoliker, F. Campbell & M. Haden, July 1987

This recommended route has sustained climbing on generally good rock. It may be better to split the last pitch to minimize rope drag. Start about 45 m north of "Peanut Dogleg" at a small tree a few metres off the ground in a short crack.

1. 50 m, 5.9. From the crack, climb easy steps up and left to a left-facing corner. Go up this to its end and then make an awkward move left to a point 10 m below the base of a large V-slot and crack system (30 m). Climb a short wall past a bolt and then step left into a hand crack. Follow this until it is possible to move onto a weakness in the steep wall on the right. Continue up to a belay on a good ledge (piton) in an alcove at the top of the wall.

2. 15 m, 5.4. Move left along the ledge and belay at two small trees.

3. 50 m, 5.10a. From the right-hand tree, climb a steep wall (5.9) and then easier ground to below a small overhang (piton). Make a tricky move right around an outside corner to a small ledge below a roof (bolt) with a smooth wall on the right. Move right and up with difficulty to a jug and climb the corner above to the top.

East Planters Wall

This fine cliff faces west and holds the sun until late in the day. There are several water streaks that may stay wet until mid-season (between "Coconut" and "Macadamia"). To date, only the obvious natural lines have been completed. Large areas of grey, water-worn rock as well as several overhanging sections remain untouched.

Approach

There are several options and all of them involve at least a little bit of scree bashing. With increased traffic a reasonable trail should become established. The normal approach is to follow the creekbed up to the canyon where the east and west walls converge and then follow a faint game trail back north along the base of the cliffs. Alternatively, a narrow gully cuts through the lower cliff bands and allows access directly to the north end of the wall. This gully also makes a convenient descent route. It is directly across from "The Scar" route on the West Wall.

The climbs are described from right to left as access is normally from the creekbed at the south end of the cliff.

Descent

The recommended descent for all climbs except "Born To Chimney" is via a fixed rappel route situated about 20 m left (north) of "Macadamia" and about 30 m right (south) of "Coconut." Two full 50 m rappels down very steep but clean rock are required to reach the ground. The first station (2 bolts) is at the right-hand (south) end of a section of smooth slabs at the edge of the cliff. The station can be tricky to reach if the rock is wet. If in doubt, walk off right as for "Born to Chimney" via easy scree slopes into the canyon where the east and west walls converge.

East Planters Wall

A. Pecan Pump (see page 52)
B. Coconut & Macadamia (see page 49)
F. Born to Chimney

East Planters Wall

Born to Chimney 175 m, 5.7
P. Stoliker & M. Brolsma, May 1987

The name speaks for itself! "Born To Chimney" was the first route climbed in Planters Valley and has been recommended to those "with a liking for caving."

The climb follows a large, right-facing chimney that begins one pitch above the ground. It climbs the right side of the large pillar/buttress formation near the south end of the cliff. Three crack lines offer access to the ledge at the base of the chimney. Begin below the centre of these, a short distance right of the chimney. See page 47.

1. 50 m, 5.6. Follow the centre crack line up to the ledge.
2. 35 m, 5.5. Move left and climb a short step into the chimney. Belay 15 m higher, at the back of the chimney just past a chockstone.
3. 40 m, 5.5. Chimney up past two large chockstones and step on to a ledge. Climb up a short step and then move back into the chimney. Follow this to a large chockstone (poor protection).
4. 50 m, 5.7. Five metres above, the chimney is blocked by another large chockstone. Pass this on the outside (5.7) and then climb over loose blocks to just below the final chimney. Move right for 5 m to an easy crack (piton), and then go up and left to the top.

**The Almond 165 m, 5.9
P. Stoliker & M. Haden, Sept. 1989

"The Almond" climbs a large left-facing corner system about 180 m north of "Born To Chimney" and about 150 m south of "Macadamia." On the right wall of the corner there is a very striking crack line that, on closer inspection, turns out to be off-width. The main corner does not extend to the ground but begins at a ledge about 25 m up the cliff with a small tree on its left side. Start at the base of the lower wall, below and slightly right of the tree, beneath a small patch of yellow rock.

1. 25 m, 5.9. Climb a steep wall on jugs, past a small patch of loose yellow rock to a bolt. Follow a flake up and right (piton) to a ledge below a short corner/crack. Climb this and continue up left to the tree. This pitch may be avoided by scrambling up from the left.
2. 50 m, 5.9. Walk right to a finger/hand crack in an open book about 5 m left of the off-width crack. Climb the open book to a ledge and then move left and climb a corner past a piton to a roof. Pull over the roof (bolt) into a niche and then move right to a widening crack on the left side of a pinnacle. Climb up for about 2 m and gain a small ledge on the steep wall to the right of the pinnacle. A couple of difficult moves on superb rock leads to a juggy face and a crack set at a more forgiving angle. Follow the crack to a two bolt belay at the top of a large pinnacle (sustained 5.9).
3. 35 m. 5.8. Move 2 m right to footholds on the wall to the right of the off-width corner-crack. Make a tricky move straight up (bolt) and then follow mostly easy ground just right of the corner/gully. Belay on the right (bolt and pitons) just before the climb steepens.
4. 55 m, 5.9. Follow the chimney/corner to the top.

Macadamia

East Planters Wall

*An Arctic Arachide 125 m, 5.10a
P. Stoliker & F. Campbell, July 1989

"AAA" follows a large left-facing corner system about 110 m north of "The Almond" and about 40 m south of "Macadamia." A steep move on the second pitch is the only difficulty on this generally easy route. The rock is solid and waterworn. Scramble up from the left to the start of good rock at the base of the corner.

1. 40 m, 5.8. Move right and climb the centre of a steep ramp, the left side of which leads to a wide crack. At about 30 m, climb a short corner/crack and then make a tricky step left to a ledge. Belay up under a roof (piton).

2. 50 m, 5.10a. Move left across a slab and climb a short step up and right. The corner ends at a steep wall broken by two crack lines and then continues above. Climb the left-hand crack (piton, 5.10a) to a belay at the top of the steep wall (piton).

3. 35 m, 5.5. Follow the corner to the top.

***Macadamia 130 m, 5.8+
P. Stoliker & F. Campbell, June 1988

"Macadamia" is one of the best climbs in Planters Valley. The rock is good and the climbing is sustained at the 5.7/5.8 level. However, the liberal use of the "+" designation should not be taken lightly. The route ends at the obvious overhanging arch at the top and in the approximate centre of the wall. A left-facing corner leads up to the right side of the arch.

The climb begins directly below the arch at a ledge with a small (2 m) tree. Scramble up for a few metres to the ledge and belay at its left end about 10 m left of the tree.

1. 45 m, 5.8+. Climb up and left across a steep wall on small holds and minimal protection to gain a ramp. Follow this up and back right to belay on a good ledge at a large flake under an overhanging wall. Alternatively, the ramp may be reached by following corners from a start lower down on the left.

2. 30 m, 5.8+. Climb the overhang above the flake (piton) and follow a corner up right. Make a tricky move left (5.8+) to gain a large ledge system and belay (pitons) directly below the prominent corner of pitch 4.

3. 30 m, 5.8. Climb the yellow corner on the right and traverse left past a piton to a good ledge. Continue up for 5 m and belay at the right-hand end of a second ledge at the base of the final corner leading up to the overhanging arch.

4. 25 m, 5.8+. Climb the corner (large gear) to a piton at the top and then swing out over the roof and up to the top of the cliff.

Frank Campbell on the spectacular, final pitch of "Macadamia" during the first ascent. Photo: Paul Stoliker.

Pecan Pump

East Planters Wall

Coconut 135 m, 5.8+
P. Stoliker & F. Campbell, Sept. 1990

"Coconut" winds its way up steep ramps and ledges about 40 m left of "Macadamia" and tops out at a notch to the left of a large yellow roof. Start below a steep, right-trending ramp.

1. 55 m, 5.6. Follow the ramp on good holds for a full rope length. Move up to a ledge and go left along the ledge to a bolt belay.
2. 40 m, 5.8. Climb an easy wall up and left for about 8 m and then go back right up a steep corner (2 pitons) to easy ground. Move left along a ledge that soon ends and then step up to another ledge and belay.
3. 40 m, 5.8+. Continue up and left for about 7 m and then move back right over loose blocks to a bolt directly above the belay. Traverse right to a corner, go up this and continue straight up on excellent rock to a fixed belay at the top (2 pitons).

***Pecan Pump 145 m, 5.10b
P. Stoliker & M. Haden, Sept. 1990

This excellent route follows a prominent left-facing corner about 120 m north of "Macadamia." It features sustained 5.8 climbing in the lower corner-crack and steep, "pumpy" face climbing higher up. The rock is reportedly excellent throughout, making the climb one of the best in Planters Valley if not the entire Ghost.

Scramble over ledges up and then right to the foot of the main corner.

1. 50 m, 5.8. Follow the corner-crack on excellent rock to a good belay (2 pitons) in a niche at the base of yellow rock. This belay can also be reached via an easier-looking ramp from the left.
2. 45 m, 5.10b. From the niche, move left and up for about 4 m to a bolt. Reach up left to a jug above a roof and make a strenuous sequence of moves up for 3 m (the "Pecan Pump"). Move back right, up and right again into a corner. Climb a short wall on the right and then follow the corner/crack up and left to a large ledge at the top of the steep climbing.

Spot the line!

Devils Gap – North Side

A. Spectre Crag
B. Wild West Wall
C. Kemp Shield
D. Bonanza
E. Ju-Jube

54

SPECTRE CRAG

This is the most westerly of the established climbing areas in Devil's Gap. Directly opposite Planters Valley there is a deep gully that breaks through the main cliff band. This is the location of the ice climbs "Aquarius" and "The Recital Hall." Located left of "Aquarius" is Spectre Crag and to the right is the Wild West Wall area of West Phantom Crag. The Spectre Crag routes are on the grey section of cliff and are visible from the parking area at the park boundary. The crag has probably not been climbed upon since the time of the first ascents and more traffic will likely establish several of the climbs as classics, particularly "Hoss" and "Spectre's Knife." No one has yet looked at the more blank sections of the cliff, some of which are very steep. Pitons are advisable for all the routes on Spectre Crag.

Approach

From the park boundary, follow the Lake Minnewanka trail west, as described in Planters Valley. After about one kilometre, instead of forking left toward the south side of the main valley, continue straight following the Gravel Trough Road to gain the riverbed near the first Ghost Lake. The lake may be dry later in the year and may also be reached by following the riverbed directly. Cross over to the north side of the river near the lake inlet and move west to the base of the "Aquarius" drainage. Hike up through fairly open trees and then move over left on easy slopes to skirt around the lower cliff band. Continue up and then left through sparsely treed, broken ground. During spring runoff, this approach may require a considerable amount of snorkeling. If so, approach by continuing west from the Wild West Wall. See page 63 for details.

Descent

For "Ponderosa Right" and "Hoss" it is possible to rappel the routes from fixed anchors. Otherwise walk right (north) along the top of the cliff to the highest point and then continue down to the north for about 100 m into a bay. Three airy rappels from conveniently placed trees lead to the base of the cliff. The first rappel is a full 50 m. See photo page 56.

Ponderosa Right 180 m, 5.9+
F. Campbell & J. A. Owen, May 1987

Seasoned Rockies climbers have given this climb one star, others have called it a little dirty. "Ponderosa Right" and "Left" start at the left end of a treed ledge about one pitch up the cliff. The ledge is reached by scrambling up easy ground on the right and then moving over left. From part way up the fourth pitch the Right or Left finish may be taken. Each is described separately.

1. 30 m, 5.7. Either climb the right-hand crack that overhangs slightly at first or follow an easier corner on the left to a fixed belay station.
2. 45 m, 5.8. Continue up a corner on the left passing a small overhang lower down to a horizontal break in the wall.
3. 15 m, 5.7. Traverse right around a buttress to an alcove with a tree and fixed belay.
4. 55 m, 5.8. Climb a break on the right side of the tree for about 10 m and then con-

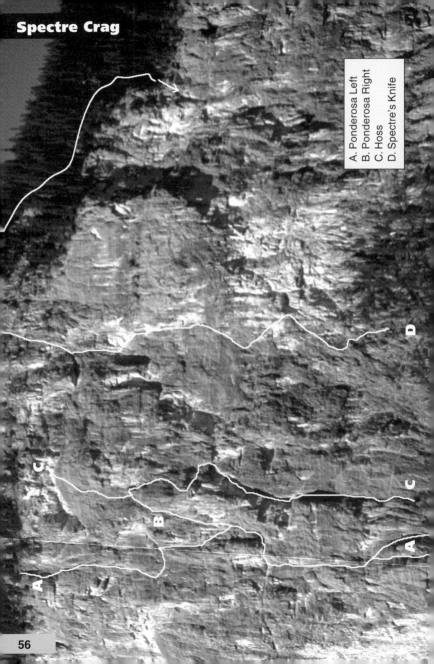

Spectre Crag

tinue up a chimney to a fixed belay almost at the top of a pinnacle. (With a 50 m rope it may be necessary for the second to begin climbing before the leader reaches the belay).

5. 35 m, 5.9+. Climb a break in the face, above and slightly left of the pinnacle, then follow a crack in the slab above to a fixed belay under an overhang just below the top.

Ponderosa Left 220 m, 5.9
F. Campbell & J. Rowe, May 1987

"Ponderosa Left" moves left and continues up to the top of the cliff from part way up pitch 4 of "Ponderosa Right."

1-3. As for "Ponderosa Right."

4. 45 m, 5.8. Climb a break on the right side of the tree for about 10 m (as for "Ponderosa Right") and then continue up and left following a crack system on good rock to a sloping ledge below overhangs.

5. 30 m, 5.6. Move down and left to gain another crack system and follow this to a belay.

6. 55 m, 5.8. Continue up the loose crack system to the top.

*Hoss 190 m, 5.9+
P. Stoliker & L. DeMarsh, Oct. 1987

"Hoss" follows a large right-facing corner topped by a huge block, just right of "Ponderosa Right." It joins that route at the top of a pinnacle, about three-quarters of the way up the cliff. The climbing is interesting and on generally good rock although two large blocks on pitch four require special care.

Start 10 m right of "Ponderosa," directly under the main corner, about 8 m below a tree growing horizontally out from a ledge.

1. 50 m, 5.7. Climb up to the tree and continue up the corner above to a ledge. Move up past a piton to a higher ledge and then go up right past a loose rock into a crack. Follow the crack until it steepens and then move up and left across a slab to a belay (bolt and piton) in the main corner.

2. 20 m, 5.8. Continue up the corner to a belay (piton and wired hex) on a ramp at the base of a wide crack in a huge corner.

3. 25 m, 5.8. With gardening tools at the ready, climb the crack for 5 m and then move right onto the face. Climb up to a bolt and then back left into the corner at the top of the steep section. Follow the corner for 5 m and move right onto the face again. Climb up to a ledge and move right and up to belay (bolt) at another ledge about 4 m below a roof and a large loose block.

4. 35 m, 5.9. Move around the roof with care and follow face holds to a bolt directly below the huge block at the top of the main corner. Pull over the block on its right, traverse left below overhangs, and climb up and left to belay on a ledge at the top of the overhangs.

Spectre Crag

5. 25 m, 5.6. Climb the crack above and follow an easy gully to the top of a pinnacle (junction with "Ponderosa") and fixed belay on the left side.

6. 35 m, 5.9+. Climb a break in the face, above and slightly left of the pinnacle, and then follow a crack in the slab above to a fixed belay under an overhang just below the top.

**Spectre's Knife 180 m, 5.8
J. A. Owen & M. McKellar, Aug. 1987

This climb starts about 50 m right of, and 25 m higher than "Ponderosa." The first pitch begins at a tree just below a small ledge with two trees growing close together. The trees are about 7 m in height and one is a "school-marm" with two trunks. The climb goes generally straight up, following a faint crack system through the blocky-looking, grey bottom section, then through yellow rock and an easily visible, short fist-crack, and finally between yellow and grey rock in a left-facing corner system to the top.

1. 45 m, 5.7. Gain the ledge above the belay and climb a crack on the right for about 3 m. Move left for about 5 m and climb up trending right in cracks and grooves until just below the yellow rock. Continue up and right to a small ledge just out of sight on the right, at the start of the yellow rock.

2. 40 m, 5.8. Move up a short distance on yellow rock and traverse left for about 5 m on small holds to a ledge at the base of the fist-crack. Climb the crack and continue up and left on face holds. Go back right over easy ground to belay.

3. 45 m, 5.7. Move straight left for about 4 m to gain a corner, go up this, and continue up following the obvious line between yellow and grey rock. Move left to belay at the base of a shattered pillar (piton).

4. 50 m, 5.8. Step left and climb the shattered pillar to the "Knife," a sharp 12 m outside corner. Climb the knife (first on the right and then on the left), and go straight up steep cracks, followed by an easy gully up and right to a tree belay at the top.

WEST PHANTOM CRAG

West Phantom Crag is the premier multi-pitch limestone crag in the Ghost if not all of Alberta. Indeed, the selection of ultra-classics is numerous, and so is the potential for new, modern routes. A straightforward approach, the southern exposure and a consistent 250-300 metre height will ensure it maintains its status for some time to come.

The cliff is one-and-a-half kilometres long and is separated into five distinct areas. They will be described from west to east: Wild West Wall (including the Arrowhead), Kemp Shield, Bonanza Area, Grey Ghost Wall and Epitaph Wall (including Spirit Pillar).

Approach

The entire West Phantom Crag is serviced by one approach. Leave your car at the Banff Park boundary in Devil's Gap. See page 36 for details to this point. Walk and/or wade downstream (west) along the riverbed. About 100 m beyond the park boundary (identified by yellow pickets) there is a treed gulch that breaks through the hillside on the right. Look for a faded, red sling on an aspen tree. Follow a trail up the gulch to where the angle lessens and it starts to curve around to the east. Hike up an intermittent trail on the steep hillside to the left. Continue into more open terrain on the crest above and follow an ever-more distinctive trail and cairns to where it diagonals left. Continue along to where the trail steepens into a scree slope about 30 m below the lower cliff band. From here it is recommended to follow a fainter side trial on the left that forms a long, switchback and rejoins the main trail higher up. This option helps avoid erosion of the scree slope and is much easier. Once back on the main trail, continue up and through the obvious break in the rock band above. This will put you directly below the right side

A. West Phantom Crag Approach
B. Phantom Bluffs Approach
1. Park Boundary

West Phantom Crag

of the Grey Ghost Wall. The routes "Southern Exposure" and "Windmills of the Mind" are looming directly above. The Grey Ghost Wall, Epitaph Wall and Phantom Tower are all reached by hiking another 50 m uphill to the cliff and following a trail at the base to your intended route(s). Bonanza Area, Kemp Shield, the Arrowhead and Wild West Wall are all found to the left by following the trail that flattens out and contours across the hillside. After 200 m or so, the trail curves into an amphitheatre known as the Bonanza Descent Gully, home of the route "Ghost Town Blues."

Bonanza Descent Gully

Of the multi-pitch routes that reach the top of the crag, only one, "Zephyr," is equipped for a rappel descent from above ("Dreams of Verdon" stops short of a loose, low-angled section leading to the top). The common descent for all other routes is down the Bonanza Descent Gully. This is located at the head of the amphitheatre between Grey Ghost Wall and "Bonanza."

To help avoid confusion, the following description will assist in finding the proper rappel point when descending from above. From the top of your route hike to the large bowl directly below the East Phantom Crag Summit. Once in the bowl, descend into a narrow scree gully. Follow this down to a level area with some large boulders. At this point the gully splits into the two grooves. The right-hand one (skiers right, looking down) is typically a flowing waterfall. Don't go down this one! The left-hand one is the proper descent. Scramble down this groove to a scree ledge with a small live tree and three dead ones. If in doubt use a belay to downclimb this section. Although you can't see it, you are on the edge of a 60 m cliff. From the live tree (bring a sling, because the rats will eat any that are left) rappel 20 m to a small stance with a cabled bolt anchor. From here a 50 m, mainly free-hanging rappel will reach the ground.

A single rope rappel is possible. Some 5 m below and to climber's left of the cabled anchor there is a chained anchor—rappel here from the tree mentioned above. A 25 m rappel will reach a second chained anchor from which there is another 25 m rappel to the ground. See the topo for "Ghost Town Blues" on page 80. If the waterfall is flowing, this option will be unequivocally unpleasant.

WILD WEST WALL

Wild West Wall marks the far west end of West Phantom Crag. It presents consistently steep and compact rock and will likely be the scene of some really hard multi-pitch routes. Several projects are underway, but owing to the extreme time, hard-work and money commitments involved, only one has been completed. Nevertheless, the handful of single pitch routes along the base and on the Arrowhead make for a fine, yet limited, sport climbing venue. Avoid the area on super-hot days. To date, all the climbs are on the south-facing wall. Another impressive wall lurks around the corner to the left over-looking the "Recital Hall/Aquarius" drainage.

Approach
Follow the West Phantom Crag approach as for the Bonanza Descent Gully. See page 59 for details. Continue west (left) along the base of the cliff on a good trail. After about 100 m the trail climbs to the side of a scree cone that marks the route "Bonanza." Continue across the scree cone, around the corner and through a patch of gnarled, bleached trees. In the open area beyond these trees is the distinct Kemp Shield. The wall left of the Kemp Shield is generally known as the Wild West Wall. The Wild West Right is everything between the Arrowhead and Kemp Shield and Wild West Left is left of the Arrowhead. The Arrowhead is the obvious detached pinnacle roughly in the middle of the wall. Wild West Wall can be reached in 10-15 minutes from the Bonanza Descent Gully (45-50 minutes from the park boundary). The routes will be described in a right to left fashion as this is the order in which you will encounter them.

Descent
All the established routes are sport climbs and have fixed stations.

Wild West Wall - Right

To date there is only one route on this section of cliff. It is found on a large thumb-shaped section of steep grey rock about halfway between the Arrowhead and Kemp Shield. Look for bolts on a face of black rock to the right of an obvious corner crack. The corner itself is unclimbed and the off-width crack on the right side of the "thumb" throws out an obvious, if not very appealing, challenge.

**Back in the Saddle 27m, 5.11a
A. Genereux & T. Pochay, June 1995

This interesting face climb was established on lead and begins the development of what appears to be a very promising piece of rock. The name spawned from the fact that this was the first route Tim Pochay did after a miraculous recovery from a serious avalanche incident on Mount Athabasca.

The Arrowhead

The Rockies are full of detached pillars similar to the Arrowhead. None, however, is known to rival the quality of this outstanding feature. Dave Morgan started on the Arrowhead in the late eighties and placed the first two bolts on what is now "Hi Ho Silver." After seeing no activity for several years on this line, Andy Genereux, with prodding from Tim Pochay, started up the route placing a bolt on lead. When it came time to place the next bolt the power drill would not operate forcing a bolder runout than anticipated to the top of the tower. The route was later retrofitted and is a classic. The main reason to finish the route, however, was to get on top and bolt an amazing overhanging arête on the north side of the tower. "Blade Runner" was finally redpointed by Pochay in September of 1993. Despite the breaking of several (non-crucial) holds, it remains the best sport route in the Ghost and has now seen several on-sight ascents.

**Solar Winds 20 m, 5.12b
T. Pochay & A. Genereux, 1994

This is technically the hardest route on the spire, if not the entire Ghost, with a devious crux sequence between the second and third bolts and sustained 11d/12a climbing above.

***Blade Runner 20 m, 5.12a
T. Pochay & A. Genereux, Sept. 1993

"The Blade" climbs the right side of the superb, clean-cut arête. The crux is low down at the first bolt with strenuous and sustained 11+ climbing to the anchor.

***Vision Quest 20 m, 5.11c
A. Genereux & T. Pochay, 1996

This companion route to "Blade Runner" climbs the arête and face to the right. The lower third is very technical and requires a variety of techniques. The remainder offers "endurance climbing" to the top.

**Hi Ho Silver 20 m, 5.10d
A. Genereux & T. Pochay , Sept. 1993

This interesting climb is harder than it looks and stays in your face all the way to the top.

The Arrowhead

THE ARROWHEAD

A	Solar Winds**	12b
B	Blade Runner***	12a
C	Vision Quest***	11c
D	Hi Ho Silver**	10d

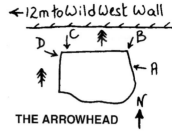

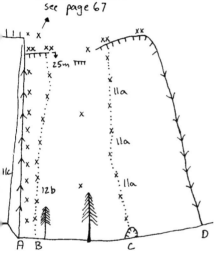

WILD WEST WALL - LEFT

A	Dreams of Verdon***	11c/d,
B	Rock Doctor**	11d
C	Gun Slingers in Paradise***	11a
D	How the West was Won	8

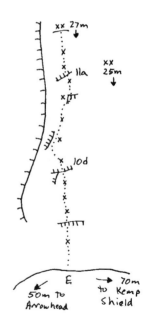

WILD WEST WALL - RIGHT

E	Back in the Saddle**	11a

Wild West Wall - Left

Three sport routes have been established on a short wall of steep grey rock that begins about 15 m west of the Arrowhead. The left-hand end of the wall is bounded by a sharp arête formed be a huge overhang that cuts deep into the cliff. A gear route "How the West Was Won" was climbed first to gain access to a ledge system some 25 m off the ground. Recently, the climb "Dreams of Verdon," which begins on the arête, was extended to the top of the crag using rap-bolting techniques. In terms of overall difficulty this is currently the hardest multi-pitch climb in the Ghost. The wall is largely composed of compact, prickly grey rock and the sport routes established here all offer excellent and sustained climbing.

***Dreams of Verdon 220 m, 5.11c/d
A. Genereux & T. Pochay, Aug. 1996

This impressive route begins on the arête below the right edge of a massive roof and continues for a total of six pitches. The rock is good throughout and the climb ranks as one of the most outstanding in Canada. Above the second pitch, two 50-metre ropes are required to descend.

Pitch two was established in a four-hour, unplanned aid fiasco. It was originally thought it might go at 5.11 but there are a few less holds than anticipated. Later the pair returned, this time from the top of the crag, and added three pitches from the top of pitch one, the second of which found easier climbing to the right of the original project. Time constraints and continued hard climbing above stalled the project for a couple of years. A final push over several days in 1996 established the last two pitches. Although every pitch has been redpointed, the route at press time has yet to see a continuous ascent.

**Rock Doctor 25 m, 5.11d
T. Pochay & A. Genereux, 1996

This fine, but somewhat squeezed route lies immediately right of "Dreams of Verdon." Although it has a separate anchor, it can be used as a variation first pitch to that route.

abandoned project
Three bolts behind the tree between "Rock Doctor" and "Gun Slingers in Paradise."

***Gun Slingers in Paradise 25 m, 5.11a
A. Genereux & T. Pochay, 1994

This route gives steep, sustained face climbing with several crux sections.

How the West was Won 25 m, 5.8
A. Genereux, 1994

This gear route, which climbs the right-facing corner at the right of the lower wall, was used to establish anchors for the other climbs. The rock is of dubious quality and the climb is probably best forgotten.

Wild West Wall - Left

WILD WEST WALL - LEFT

Dreams of Verdon*** 220 m, 11c/d
16QDs, incl. long slings

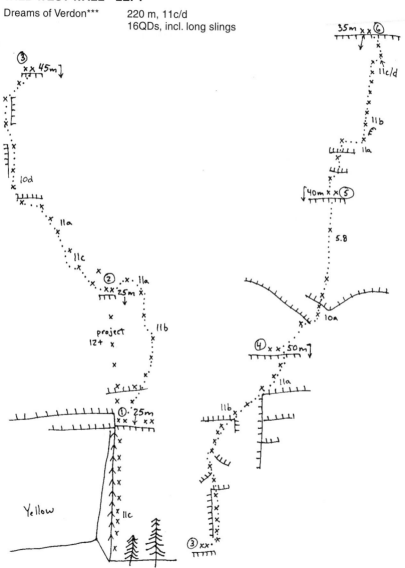

KEMP SHIELD

Situated at the base of a tremendous 300 metre wall, this is a most unique feature. Centuries of water pouring off the summit overhangs have etched an immaculate slab of compact stone surrounded by overhanging yellow rock. The slab is named in memory of the late Dennis Kemp who on a visit from England during the summer of 1986 helped Dave Morgan pioneer several routes in the Ghost.

Kemp Shield suffers from unusually finicky conditions. In the spring and during rainy periods, it is hopelessly wet from water running off the top of the crag. During hot spells, you will roast or die from heat exhaustion. There are no trees to provide shade and the overhanging walls contribute an albedo effect that adds to the already inciting black rock. Early summer and fall are good times to check out these routes.

The lack of features make what few routes have been done unusually technical. Because there has been little climbing activity in the past, some of the routes are dirty; remnants of the constant water battering. With more traffic, the routes would undoubtedly clean up. Despite some impressive efforts, large expanses of unclimbed rock remain and the area holds plenty of interest for future exploration.

Of the eight routes produced to date, all were established by Ghost pioneer Dave Morgan. Most of them are above average and the crag is a recommended destination for a day. Many of the hangers here are homemade and require small profile carabiners. See the "fixed protection" section of the introduction on page 11.

Climbs have been established in two separate sections of the cliff, one just left of centre and the other at the right-hand end. See photos pages 60, 68 and 74 and accompanying topos pages 71 and 73.

Approach

The Kemp Shield is an obvious apron of dark rock located between "Bonanza" and Wild West Wall. It is reached in 5-10 minutes from the Bonanza Descent Gully or 40-45 minutes from the park boundary. See the West Phantom Crag introduction on page 59 for more approach details.

Descent

All routes are descended by rappel, many requiring two 45 m ropes.

Kemp Shield - Left Side

The section on the left consists essentially of one major route, "Big Rock Traditional," and its two variations, "Shred" and "Fool's Gold." These climbs are best located by a prominent ledge about 12 m above the ground and about 20 m left of the lowest point at the base of the cliff.

*Big Rock Traditional 70 m, 5.10c
D. Morgan, B. Huseby & K. Hines, 1991

This interesting climb was established in traditional style, with all the bolts being drilled by hand and on-lead. The route required a number of attempts spread over two years and much patience from Dave Morgan's wife Bev who belayed him on many of them.

Begin directly below a short groove that leads to the prominent ledge noted above. The first bolt is a long way up and steady climbing is required to reach it. Technical but protected climbing then leads up past a second bolt and the groove to the ledge. From here, traverse right and up to a ramp that angles rightwards to a small ledge and chained anchors. The second pitch climbs the steep wall on the left to a short groove and belay ledge above. The upper part of the shield is lower angled and the route does not continue beyond this point.

*Shred 15 m, 5.12a
D. Morgan, B. Wyvill & G. Powter, 1993

A short, technical route that climbs the wall a few metres right of "Big Rock Traditional." It gains the right end of a small ledge system extending out from the top of the groove.

**Fool's Gold 40 m, 5.11c/d
D. Morgan & T. Freeman, 1990

This very technical route follows a faint, ochre-tinted streak that leads directly to the belay at the top of pitch one on "Big Rock Traditional." The technical crux is low down but the bolts seem widely spaced higher up as you near the anchor. It makes an excellent route when combined with the second pitch of "Big Rock Traditional."

Kemp Shield - Left Side

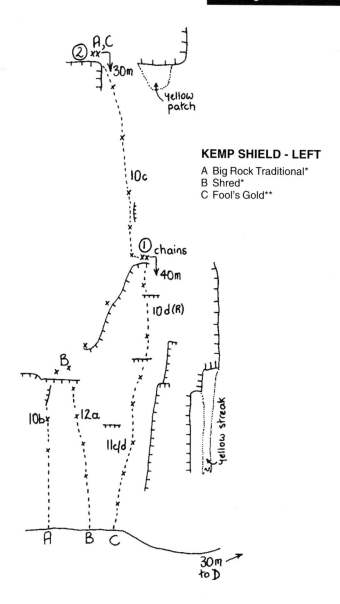

KEMP SHIELD - LEFT

A	Big Rock Traditional*	70 m, 10c
B	Shred*	12a
C	Fool's Gold**	11c/d

71

Kemp Shield - Right Side

Climbs on the right-hand section of the cliff are described from right to left as this is the normal direction of approach. The far right-end of the Shield is marked by an obvious right-facing corner at the boundary of grey and yellow rock.

*Boldly Go 45 m, 5.10c/d
D. Morgan, B. Huseby, T. Jones, E. Trouillot & A. Pickel, 1990

This enjoyable and well-protected route climbs a thin finger crack in the centre of a flat, poorly-defined pinnacle located above ledges about 20 m up the face. The start of the route is about 18 m left of the extreme right end of the Shield, below a shallow groove that begins about 6 m up the face and leads over left to the base of the upper crack. The crack requires a good selection of small gear.

User Friendly 45 m, 5.9
D. Morgan, B. Huseby & A. Skuce, 1990

"User Friendly" climbs the left-facing corner on the left side of the upper pinnacle of "Boldly Go." It is entirely bolt-protected except for one large gear placement at the top of the offwidth crack in the corner (#3.5-4 Friend). The addition of a bolt at this point is recommended to make the climb match its name. The climb begins about 5 m left of "Boldly Go" and goes up to the ledge system below the upper corner via a V-shaped alcove in the lower wall.

Tradesman's Entrance 50 m, 5.8
D. Morgan & B. Huseby, Aug 1986

This route was originally used to access the upper part of the Shield and to place the bolts on "Scaremonger" and "Cryin' Mercy." It begins about 10 m left of "User Friendly" and just right of a prominent, right-facing corner that begins a few metres above the ground. Move up and left past a bolt (5.8) to the corner, and go up this moving right at the top over small ledges (bolt high up on left) to the base of a crack in a second right-facing corner (bolt). Climb the steep corner (gear to 2") until it closes at a ledge on the right. Move up on to the ledge and step right (crux) to easier ground. Continue up past a bolt and climb an easy corner to a bolt belay and chains on a flat-topped block.

*Scaremonger 50 m, 5.10c R
D. Morgan, B. Huseby & D. Kemp, Aug, 1986

This aptly named route climbs a shallow crack in the steep face above and slightly left of the lower corner of "Tradesman's Entrance." The crack is difficult to protect and a good selection of small/medium gear is recommended. Climb "Tradesman's Entrance" as far as the bolt at the top of the lower corner. From here, move up and left with difficulty around a bulge to a bolt and continue left to the base of the shallow crack. Follow the crack moving right and up at the top to a short, right-facing corner. This leads up to the rappel anchors at the flat-topped block of "Tradesman's Entrance." At the top of the crack it is tempting to move right on to "Tradesman's Entrance" and the addition of a bolt at this point is recommended to encourage use of the original finish.

Kemp Shield - Right Side

***Cryin' Mercy 45 m+, 5.11a/b
D. Morgan & B. Huseby, Sept. 1987

"Cryin' Mercy" is the best route on the Kemp Shield to date. It typifies what the crag has to offer—steep, continuously technical face climbing on excellent rock. The route has several difficult sections and the location of the crux seems to be a matter of opinion. Begin a few metres left of the lower corner of "Tradesman's Entrance" and angle up left following the line of bolts. The route continues up the steep face and exits up a right-facing groove. The upper part is runout but relatively easy.

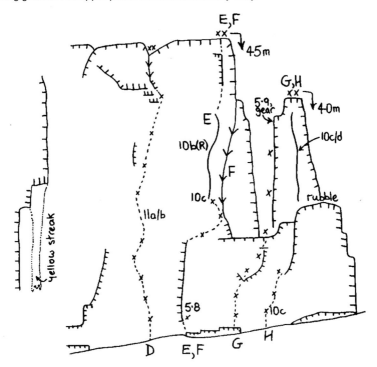

KEMP SHIELD - RIGHT

D Cryin' Mercy***	11a/b	
E Scaremonger*	10c R	small-med wires, TCUs
F Tradesman's Entrance	8	
G User Friendly	9	med-large wires
H Boldly Go*	10c/d	small wires

Wild West Wall & Bonanza

A. Kemp Shield
B. Bonanza
C. Ju-Jube

74

BONANZA AREA

This area lies between the Descent Gully and the Kemp Shield. Only one climb goes to the top of the main crag and it checks in near the top of the list for THE outstanding rock route in the Canadian Rockies. This, of course, is the ultra-classic "Bonanza."

The first ascent of the climb was rather uneventful except they couldn't believe just how good the crack was and they kept yelling down to each other about their fortune. The infamous traverse was discovered simply by going around the corner "for a look." Soon they spied the foot ledge leading back right and the big holds just kept coming.

To get off the climb, they then headed down what is now called the Bonanza Descent Gully. Knowing that the rappel would be tight with only 45 m ropes, they downclimbed to the lip (site of the present cable anchor) and as they threw the ropes it was getting dark, raining hard and the ropes just disappeared into space. Chris Perry launched over the edge with nothing more than "two small bootlace-sized pieces of nylon" to use as prussiks as a last resort. He could only see about halfway down the cliff and the ropes didn't reach the ground but he was encouraged by the fact that at least they were laying on easier-angled rock. At the bottom of the ropes, a pendulum right and a jump onto the rising scree slope turned a potential epic into just another day in the Ghost.

Approach

All three routes in this area are listed relative to "Bonanza." Approach as for the rest of West Phantom Crag and the Descent Gully. See page 59. Continue west (left) past the Descent Gully for about 200 m to an obvious scree cone. Partway up this scree cone there is a prominent chimney that forms the left side of a large 45 m pinnacle. This is the start to "Bonanza." A fourth route, "Ghost Town Blues," is found in the Descent Gully between "Bonanza" and the Grey Ghost Wall.

Descent

Hike right across scree and around the corner to less exposed tree slopes on the east-facing bowl above the Descent Gully. Traverse the slope to the right toward the back of the bowl. Cross the first small gully/stream (this ends in a steep waterfall) and continue right into the next major scree system. Follow this down and into the Descent Gully. See page 61 and topo page 80 for the remaining details.

Rock n' Robin 35 m, 5.9
T. Jones & R. Stark, Aug. 1991

About 75 m left of the start of "Bonanza" where the path starts to descend the scree slope there is a short, left-facing corner that starts about 7 m up the cliff and leads to a ledge with a small tree on the right.

Beginning below and left of the corner, climb the slabby right wall of a short groove and continue up right to the base of the corner. Go up this past an old piton (crux) and continue up the crack with excellent protection to a stance at the tree on the right. Rappel from the tree.

Bonanza Area

BONANZA AREA

A Bonanza***	260 m, 8	stnd rack, extra 2-3"
A' Bonanza Direct	60 m, 10a	Bonanza rack + 2-3 pins

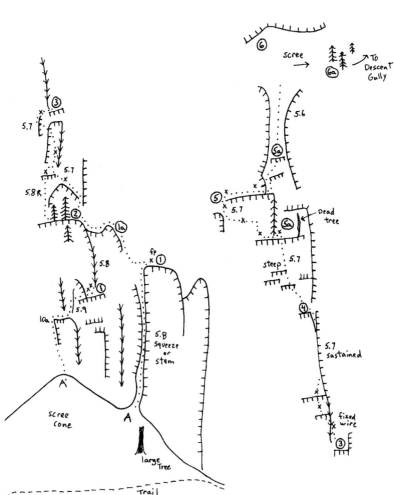

Bonanza Area

***Bonanza 260 m, 5.8
C. Perry & M. White, June 1976

"Bonanza" lies in the only major corner line left of the Descent Gully. West Phantom Crag makes an uncharacteristic bend at this corner and as a result, "Bonanza" faces almost due east. Accordingly, it loses the sun much earlier in the day than the rest of the cliff. In the right light, the splitter crack in the middle of the climb is easily seen in the back of the corner. Such sustained and relatively uniform cracks are a rarity in local limestone. And the devious traverse near the top adds spice and will challenge your rope work. Enough said, have fun....

There are many different ways to piece together the pitches and everyone we talk to seems to have the best way. There are numerous stances with good natural cracks. The belays indicated on the topo are only one option and are for reference only. Use your own judgment based on the length of your cord and the rope drag you encounter. Pitons are not necessary.

1. 45 m, 5.8. Climb the left-facing chimney, which is easy at first and then turns steep and narrow. There are two possible ways to attack the wide crack that is probably the crux of the climb; either stem across it or squeeze into it. Take your pick.

2. 30 m, 5.7. From the top of the pinnacle (piton), traverse left on a small foot ledge to a corner. Go up this and across left to a tree belay on the large ledge below the upper corner.

3. 35 m, 5.7. A subsidiary groove on the right (directly behind tree belay) is followed for about 10 m before a traverse diagonally left can be made into the main corner. Interesting climbing on good rock leads to a small stance.

4 & 5. 100 m, 5.7. Follow the steep and sustained corner for two 50 m pitches to a ledge below the obvious overhang in the upper section of the corner (piton on the right). There is a small dead tree on this ledge.

6. 50 m, 5.7. Traverse left around an outside corner and onto the face. Follow small but good holds across (pitons) to a small corner and go up this to a ledge with two pins. Follow a good foot ledge back right (piton) to the main corner. Either belay here or continue up to a higher ledge and belay there. Long slings and two ropes are useful on this pitch.

6. alt. Alternatively, you can split the traverse by belaying at the ledge with two pins before moving back right to the main corner. A 35 m pitch from here will reach the top.

7. 5.6. An easier pitch leads to a scree slope at the top. The length depends upon where you belay at the end of pitch 6. The top belay requires some ingenuity, but can usually be found in the rotten cliff band above the scree slope. If not, traverse right to trees.

Note: The authors have heard rumours that at least one party has avoided the traverse on pitch 6 by climbing directly up the corner and over the large roof. We also heard it was rated 5.9. Considering the activity the route has seen over the years, it is very likely that it has been climbed. It is also very likely that 5.9 is a sandbag.

Bonanza

Bonanza Direct 60 m, 5.10a
F. Campbell, D. Stefani & N. Stefani, July 1994

A better name for this route might be "Bonanza Indirect." The first pitch involves a major traverse and is hard to protect without pitons. It was also originally graded 5.8+! The fixed piton belay at the top of pitch one provides the final rappel point for parties backing off "Bonanza."

The route starts just to the left of the top of the scree cone and below an obvious left-corner about 10 m off the ground. From the top of the corner move across right to a larger corner system that leads to the traverse on pitch 2 of the normal route.

1. 30 m, 5.10a. Climb a faint break in the slab that leads to the corner and climb the corner (15 m). From the top of the corner (some loose rock) traverse right across a small bay of compact rock to thin crack on the right wall. Climb up the crack for 3-4 m to where a small ledge leads right to a larger belay ledge (pitons).

2. 30 m, 5.8. Climb the corner directly above to join the normal route on the easy traverse leading left. Follow this and belay on the treed ledge.

Above: Nicky LePage atop the first pitch of "Bonanza."
Photo: Joe Josephson.
Opposite: Martyn White crossing the infamous pitch six traverse during the first ascent of "Bonanza." Photo: Chris Perry.

Bonanza Descent Gully

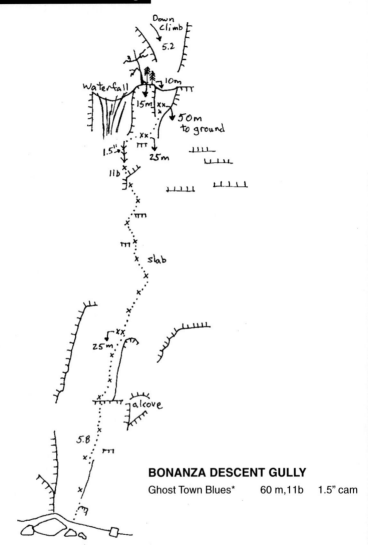

BONANZA DESCENT GULLY

Ghost Town Blues* 60 m, 11b 1.5" cam

Bonanza Descent Gully

*Ghost Town Blues 60 m, 5.11b
K. Haberl, R. Jaeger & D. Orr, 1994

"Ghost Town Blues" was first done strictly as an access to the top of the crag. Beyond knowing who bolted it, it is unclear who actually first redpointed the thing. The climb is wet until mid-season and when dry, the bottom is dirty but still worth doing if you are in the area. The first 5.8 pitch (25 m) can be done on its own or continue up the second 5.11b pitch, which has sustained climbing in the upper half.

An early attempt at "Ghost Town Blues" in poor conditions. Photo: Trevor Jones.

Grey Ghost Wall

This section of cliff is named for obvious reasons. It presents a uniform-looking wall that is some 200 m to 300 m high and almost solid grey throughout. Naturally, it has a high concentration of quality, multi-pitch climbs. It is bounded on the left by the Bonanza Descent Gully and on the right by huge, stepped overhangs of yellow rock that extend almost the entire height of the crag. The Grey Ghost Wall itself can be separated into two parts by the left-slanting diagonal break of the route "Grey Ghost." To its left the cliff is somewhat shorter and more broken and to its right there is a steep slab of sweeping, compact rock. If you were to climb on only one multi-pitch venue in the Ghost, this would be it. Every route except for "Helmet Crack" and "Grey Ghost" is highly recommended. However, it seems to date that only "Zephyr" (two ascents), "Banshee" (two ascents), "Windmills of the Mind" (three ascents) and "Southern Exposure" (numerous ascents) have been repeated.

Approach
See the West Phantom Crag introduction on page 59 for details. The trail nears the base of the cliff directly below the route "Southern Exposure." When the trail contours left toward the Bonanza Descent Gully, continue straight up for 50 m to the base of the crag. It is about a 45 minute hike from the parking area at the park boundary.

Descent
The standard descent is to hike left (west) and rappel the Bonanza Descent Gully. See page 61 for details.

"Zephyr" is the only route on the crag that is equipped for a rappel descent. Since "Banshee" and "Grey Ghost" both end at the top anchor, it is recommended to use this rappel line. This can also be used as a descent from other Grey Ghost Wall or Epitaph Wall routes. As you hike west along the top of the crag toward the Descent Gully, you will encounter an easy slab approximately in the middle of the Grey Ghost Wall. Near the bottom of the slab is the only pine tree in the vicinity. The top anchor of "Zephyr" is found at the edge of the cliff in a shallow gully formation just below (west) the tree and slab. It is advised that you climb "Zephyr" to figure out where this rappel line is located and if in doubt use the Bonanza Descent Gully.

Helmet Crack 180 m, 5.8
J. Firth & J. Upton, June 1979

About 150 m right of the Bonanza Descent Gully near the top of a scree slope and immediately left of two large pinnacles at the base of the cliff there is a deep corner leading up to a gully in the upper part of the cliff. The climb follows the corner all the way and is mainly 5.6 with a 5.8 roof near the top.

Grey Ghost Wall

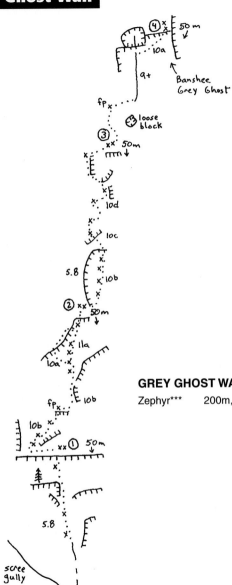

GREY GHOST WALL

Zephyr***   200m, 11a   12 QDs, gear to 3"

Grey Ghost Wall

***Zephyr 200 m, 5.11a
A. Genereux & J. Josephson, July 1995

The first ascent of this route was completed in a single afternoon with rapidly waning battery power. The name was applied two days later as the team used the route as a descent from the first ascent of "Windmills of the Mind." While setting up the top rappel, a violent gust of wind ripped a jet-black jacket out of Josephson's pack. The now-air-borne coat filled with air and took on a humanoid appearance as it briefly hovered 30 metres out—taunting the climbers before heading out of sight in the general direction of Calgary. It was just another Ghost climbing experience.

"Zephyr" is a modern route that climbs the right side of a wide, dished corner system left of "Grey Ghost." It is possible to follow the base of the cliff left from "Southern Exposure," however, this entails a healthy scree bash. It is better to follow the trail west as for the Descent Gully for 150 m or so to a point directly below some large, detached pinnacles and blocks. Scramble up the talus and around the right end of the blocks and into a scree gully. "Zephyr" begins in an irregular crack about halfway up this gully. Scamper onto the blocks; the first few bolts are easily seen on a clean wall above the crack.

1. 50 m, 5.8. Climb a shallow, intermittent crack in good grey rock to two bolts on a face to the left. Climb the face to avoid the bad rock in the corner to the right. More broken ground passes a ledge with a small tree. Continue up and past a bolt to a large ledge and a bolt belay.

2. 50 m, 5.11a. Move left along the ledge and climb up past two bolts (10b), then continue on excellent rock up and right past a bolt and a fixed piton to gain a shallow corner. Climb the corner (10c) for 10 m and exit left onto the face. Climb up with increasing difficulty past four bolts (11a) with an easier, variation escape to the left at the second bolt (10b). Continue up to easier ground that leads past a bolt to a bolt belay below a large left-facing corner.

3. 50 m, 5.10d. Continue up the corner (5.8) or climb out right past four bolts on excellent, textured rock (10b). Both options arrive at a large ledge. Face climb on awkward moves past three bolts. At the third bolt traverse right (10d) for 3 m and climb past a bolt moving left into shallow corner (10c). Climb the shallow groove and after several metres exit right past a bolt to a bolt belay.

4. 50 m, 5.10a. Face climb up and left to avoid a loose block on the right. Continue up and right past a fixed pin to gain a prominent finger and hand crack. Climb the crack (5.9+) for 30 m to below a shattered block. Traverse right for 3 m and climb an awkward corner (10a) to the top and a bolt belay.

Grey Ghost Wall

*Banshee 180 m, 5.10a
P. Littlejohn & I. Staples, Sept. 1976

Banshee climbs the well-featured terrain between "Zephyr" and "Grey Ghost." The upper section of the latter route forms the right side of a shallow pinnacle with a well-defined corner system on its left side. "Banshee" climbs this left-side corner system to the top of the pinnacle and then finishes up "Grey Ghost." Pitons would be an excellent idea for this route.

The original route starts left of "Zephyr." Approach as for that route and scramble up the scree gully behind the pinnacles and locate a 4th class ledge system that leads out right. This system crosses "Zephyr" at the first belay (bolts) and extends all the way to "Grey Ghost" (some 5th class). Traverse easily right past "Zephyr" for about 12 m until below and slightly left of the upper corner and then move up to belay on a large ledge. The first pitch of "Zephyr" would make an excellent alternate start.

1. 40 m, 5.7. Climb straight up for 10 m and then use a detached ledge to traverse right to a groove. Climb the left-hand option and continue past a short V-groove to a ledge about 10 m below where the crack steepens.

2. 45 m, 5.10a. Climb up to a piton below the bulge and continue up with difficulty into the corner above. An easy groove leads up and left to a belay behind some big blocks, well left of the main groove line.

3. 30 m, 5.8. Steep climbing bearing right leads to ledges. Climb down to the foot of an easy corner on the right and follow this to a stance beneath the conspicuous left-slanting corner.

4. 15 m, 5.7. Climb the corner to a bolt belay at the top of the pinnacle.

5. 50 m, 5.7. Climb the slabby groove above and continue up a left-trending corner with a steep move at the top. Finish at the top anchor of "Zephyr." **Note:** the first ascent team of "Zephyr" found the exit move to be 10a.

Grey Ghost 255 m, 5.8+
J. Firth & T. Jones, Sept. 1976

This route follows the left-slanting diagonal break in the centre of the cliff. It was originally titled "Rattling Corner." This name should tell you what you're in for. If this route were on Yam, it would undoubtably clean up and be a classic. Start at an easy ramp and ledge system that leads out right to ledges at the base of a shallow corner. The ramp is well down the scree slope from the start of "Banshee" and 60-70 m left of the start of "Southern Exposure." Scramble up and right to the base of the corner, about 10 m above the ground. Take pitons.

1. 35 m, 5.5. Climb the corner and then the arête on the right to a bolt belay.

2. & 3. 80 m, 5.5. Continue easily trending left up a series of short steps and corners to a block belay where the climbing steepens (bolt).

4. 40 m, 5.8+. Either climb directly up the corner (5.8+) or traverse right after 6 m past a cracked block to another crack system and follow this until a traverse leads back left to the main corner (5.7). Continue up to the foot of a chimney.

Grey Ghost Wall

5. 50 m, 5.8. Climb the chimney to the top of the pinnacle.
6. 50 m, 5.8+. Continue as for pitch 5 of Banshee. **Note:** the first ascent team of "Zephyr" found the exit move to be 10a.

**Mantissa 265 m, 5.9+
C. Yonge & J. Rollins, Oct. 1983

"Mantissa" is a nice outing on excellent rock with a couple of really rompy, juggy pitches at an easier grade lower down. The climbing higher up is sustained and bold. This brilliant if not slightly serious route pieces together natural lines without using bolts (they didn't even take any, "Business as usual!" said Yonge)—testimony to a rapidly waning ethic. Take pitons and a good selection of gear. Also, you can pretty much go to the bank and say the stated grade is rather soft.

1. 45 m, 5.5. Climb the first pitch of "Grey Ghost" to a bolt belay. Continue past the belay to a large ledge on the right.
2. 45 m, 5.7. Climb up to a groove that leads up to a prominent block below the steep face. The block is level with and left of a steep, grey, slabby section capped by small overhangs.
3. 45 m, 5.9+. Traverse left toward "Grey Ghost" until it is possible to climb a shallow groove. Continue up past the end of the alternative traverse on pitch 4 of "Grey Ghost" to a belay on the right at the base of a system of cracks through the grey wall above. John Rollins felt this is the crux pitch and recommended the addition of **one** bolt.

John Rollins on the landmark first ascent of "Mantissa."
Photo: Chas Yonge.

Grey Ghost Wall

4. 45 m, 5.8. Climb the first crack for a short distance, traverse right to a second, and continue up and right to a third. Continue straight up the wall on excellent rock to a belay in a bottomless, right-facing corner.

5. 40 m, 5.9+. From the top of the corner, climb a crack trending slightly left to gain a face and then a faint crack system that leads up through a steep bulge (difficult to protect—recommended **one** bolt addition). Belay in a niche above.

6. 45 m, 5.9. Go up and right to a piton. Continue face climbing trending back left to a right-facing corner directly above the stance and follow this to the top.

*Ziggurat 290 m, 5.10a
C. Perry & C. Dale, Sept. 1983

"Ziggurat" moves out farther right than "Mantissa" on to the steep grey wall and has a difficult and committing crux section through a compact bulge at about two-thirds height. Another classic in the traditional style. Be sure to include a healthy diet of iron (pitons).

The first ascentionist continued along the "Banshee" traverse to reach "Grey Ghost" and then climbed up to the alternate traverse on pitch 4 of that route. It is recommended, however, to use the first three pitches of "Mantissa."

1. 45 m, 5.5. Climb the first pitch of "Grey Ghost" and continue past the bolt belay to a large ledge on the right.

2. 45 m, 5.7. Climb up to a groove that leads up to a prominent block below the steep face. The block is level with and left of a steep grey slabby section capped by small overhangs.

3. 45 m, 5.8. Traverse left toward "Grey Ghost" until it is possible to move up a shallow groove. Continue past the end of the alternative traverse on pitch 4 of "Grey Ghost" to a belay on the right at the base of a system of cracks through the grey wall above.

4. 45 m, 5.7. Climb the first crack for a short distance, traverse right to a second, and continue up and right to a third. At this point "Mantissa" heads straight up the wall. "Ziggurat" continues up and diagonally right on good rock to ledges below a bulge in the wall.

5. 10 m. A short pitch leads up left to a belay immediately below the bulge.

6. 30 m, 5.10a. Climb a short corner and move out right past a piton to make a difficult move over an overlap on to the slabby wall above. Continue up and then right to a shallow groove.

7. 10 m. Climb up the groove to reach a better belay.

8. 40 m, 5.8. Continue up the wall above moving over left near the top to belay in a right-facing corner.

9. 20 m. Continue up the corner and move out right to finish.

Grey Ghost Wall

***Southern Exposure 300 m, 5.11a
T. Pochay & A. Genereux, Sept. 1993

This was completed over two days in somewhat marginal weather. All climbing was established on-lead with the Hilti drill carried by the leader. Several bolts were drilled off hooks and fixed ropes were employed to gain the upper pitches on the second day. As well, Andy was at work earning his wings when he blew a hook for a 25 footer on the last pitch.

This climb offers some excellent climbing and has become an instant classic. Later climbers found a 5.8 system to the right that avoids the final crux pitch. Why anyone would forsake the final pitch for any reason other than bad weather remains a mystery. The second half of the final pitch presents one of the finest positions imaginable on impeccable rock. It is the most memorable pitch on the climb.

"Southern Exposure" is the first route you encounter once you scramble up the hill from the trail. It starts in a yellow groove leading to an overhang with a large right-facing corner above. There is a hard-to-see, homemade bolt hanger just below the first roof. There is usually a cairn built on some flat rocks at the base of the route.

1. 47m, 5.10c. Climb a shallow left-facing corner for several metres and make a move left and then go up past a bolt (10c). Climb the left-leaning corner above and exit right at the roof (10a) and wander up and right to a belay.

2. 48m, 10a. Take the corner directly above the belay for 5 m and then move left onto a face and climb up past a bolt (10a) to broken ground. Take the left of two large corners and climb a steep, wide tower past a bolt to a large ledge and a belay.

3. 15 m, easy 5th. Climb the stepped corner up and right to a large ledge and a belay.

4. 35 m, 5.11a. Face climb directly up from the belay past two bolts. Make difficult moves left (11a) to gain a steep and exposed ramp. Climb the ramp (10c) and exit left over a lip to a belay.

5. 50 m, 5.10b. Face climb up and left past two bolts. Move out right from the second bolt and go up through an overlap and move back left to a bolt (10b). Climb up and left and into a shallow corner with a fixed pin. From the pin climb a rising traverse right to a belay.

6. 50 m, 10a. Move up and right to gain a ledge. Work back left along the ledge until it is possible to gain a shallow corner. Climb the corner for 30 m and exit up and right (10a) to a belay.

7. 50 m, 5.11a. Climb an obvious left-facing corner for 20 m until it is possible to gain the superb headwall. Face climb up the gently overhanging wall past seven bolts to a belay just below the top. Scramble up to the scree and walk off to the Descent Gully.

Grey Ghost Wall

GREY GHOST WALL

Southern Exposure***   300 m, 11a   12 QDs, gear to 2.5"

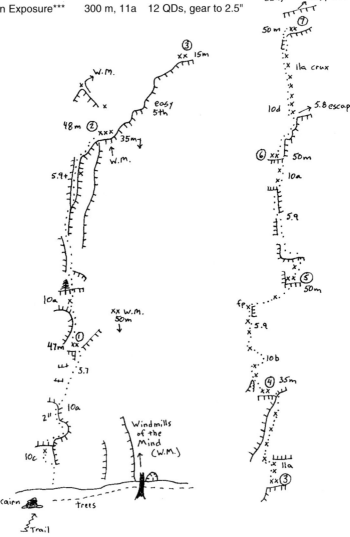

Grey Ghost Wall

GREY GHOST WALL

Windmills of the Mind*** 300 m, 11b 12 QDs, gear to 3"

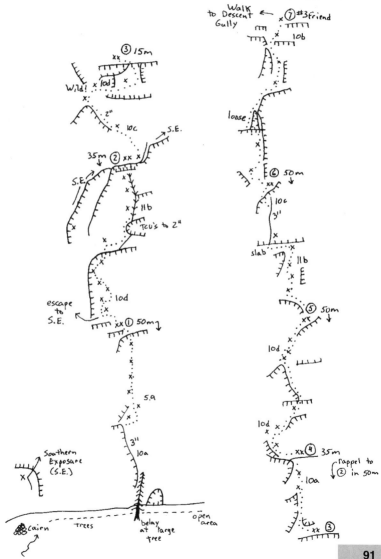

Grey Ghost Wall

***Windmills of the Mind 300 m, 5.11b
A. Genereux & J. Josephson, July 1995

The first pitch of this route was done by Brian Gross and Choc Quinn with only one bolt some eight years earlier just after their ascent of "Creamed Cheese." The pair then traversed left onto what is now the second pitch of "Southern Exposure" and followed that line to their high point near the start of the 5.11 climbing on pitch four. It was an impressive and bold effort as they carried only "five or six bolts."

After his ascent of "Southern Exposure," Andy Genereux climbed the original pitch in its single-bolt, ground-fall state. Permission from Gross and a Hilti gun has since created the start to one of the finest and sustained routes in the area.

"Windmills" is more sustained than its neighbour "Southern Exposure" and has some difficult sections requiring gear. It was done from the ground up except for the second pitch, which was put in on rappel but not top roped. All bolts were drilled from natural stances without using hooks. The first six belays are equipped for rappel. The top anchor is a single bolt next to a perfect #3 Friend crack.

The route starts directly behind a large tree some 20 m right of "Southern Exposure." It is easily identified by a splitter hand-crack in a right-facing corner.

1. 50 m, 5.10a. Start up the corner with an excellent hand crack (10a). When the corner peters out, traverse right past a bolt to another older bolt. Climb up and then left to gain a shallow corner. Climb the corner and exit left to the belay.

2. 35 m, 5.11b. Wander up the face trending left (10d) to a ledge. Move right to gain a steep corner and climb past a bulge (TCUs to 2") to a bolt (11b). Battle upwards through an overhang that joins the belay ledge shared with "Southern Exposure."

3. 15 m, 5.10d. Make several awkward moves to gain a small dihedral directly above the belay. Continue up the dihedral to a bolt and make several exposed moves up and right (10d), traversing to a small corner that is followed to the belay ledge.

4. 35 m, 5.10a. Move left to gain a shallow right-facing corner and climb the corner (10a) to gain a large ledge and a belay. You can rappel pitches 3 and 4 together.

5. 50 m, 5.10d. Traverse left along the ledge for 5 m and climb up. At the second bolt make difficult moves right on slightly crumbly rock and then up to a bolt. Climb up past a small bulge to a ledge and a shallow right-facing corner. Climb the corner to gain a pedestal. Thin moves on a bulletproof face lead right to a crack and a belay.

6. 50 m, 5.11b. Climb up and left along a ramp and make several hard moves to a lieback flake on the right (large wire). Move left and delicately climb up on great rock (11b) to gain a rounded ledge below an overlap. A traverse left leads into a spectacular hand crack. Climb the crack (10c) for 30 m to a belay.

7. 50 m, 5.10b. Face climb left and up to a bolt. Move up and right into a left-facing corner. Climb the corner making hard moves left while below a large detached pinnacle (loose). Climb back into the corner and gently pass the pinnacle to a large ledge. Face climb up to a shallow corner that leads to the top (10b) and a single bolt belay with a perfect #3 Friend crack.

Epitaph Wall

A. Creamed Cheese
B. Prosopopoeia

Creamed Cheese

Al Pickel sorting out the routefinding crux (pitch 3) of "Creamed Cheese" during the second ascent. Photo: Trevor Jones.

EPITAPH WALL

The large stepped corner on the right side of Grey Ghost Wall defines the left edge of this wall; Phantom Tower defines the eastern end. This wall is dedicated to passing friends. May their spirit and dreams stay with us.

Epitaph Wall has large sections of what appears to be rotten, overhanging yellow rock. Subsequently, it is home to fewer routes than its neighbouring Grey Ghost Wall. The three full-length routes are, however, some of the few routes that can compete with the Grey Ghost Wall in quality. All are superb and must-dos.

Approach
See page 59 for details getting to the base of the cliff. Follow a trail right (east) from the base of the Grey Ghost Wall to a short scree slope that ends near the start of "Creamed Cheese." Near the top of the slope there is a small detached pillar that marks the left side of the Spirit Pillar area. "The Wraith" is another 80 m right of the detached pillar and 50 m left of the deep gully that separates Epitaph Wall from Phantom Tower. The crag is reached in 45-50 minutes from the car.

Descent
Walk left and use the Bonanza Descent Gully. See page 61 for details.

***Creamed Cheese 310 m 5.11a
B. Gross & C. Quinn, Aug. 1987

This monumental route was first started by Brian Gross, Choc Quinn and David Cheesmond. The trio made several efforts and reached the top of pitch four before David was lost while attempting the Hummingbird Ridge on Mount Logan. The remaining pair, along with Al Pickel, sorted out the fifth pitch on the penultimate attempt. Gross and Quinn returned to polish off the route, which included the spectacular sixth pitch. The pair wanted to name the route the "Dave Cheesmond Memorial" until Gillian, David's widow, christened the route "Creamed Cheese." Pitches 4, 5 and 6 have several options as to where to belay. The description below is that taken on the first ascent and includes several single bolt anchors. The topo on page 96 shows a second option that eliminates one pitch and helps avoid the inadequate anchors. The route is regularly done without pitons, although a few knifeblades and the occasional angle might be welcome.

The route starts about 20 m left of the detached pillar that identifies the Spirit Pillar area. Look for a large blocky ledge system 10 m off the ground that leads left to an obvious right-facing chimney.

The first ascent party rappelled the route from single bolt anchors at the top of pitches 8, 6, 4 and 2. This is not a good option at any time, and especially not after the bolts are nearly 10 years old. Do not attempt to rappel the route. Descend the Bonanza Descent Gully.

1. 45 m, 5.6. Several options lead up to a blocky ledge system that gains access to a large right-facing chimney. Climb the chimney to a large ledge directly below the big yellow corner.

Creamed Cheese

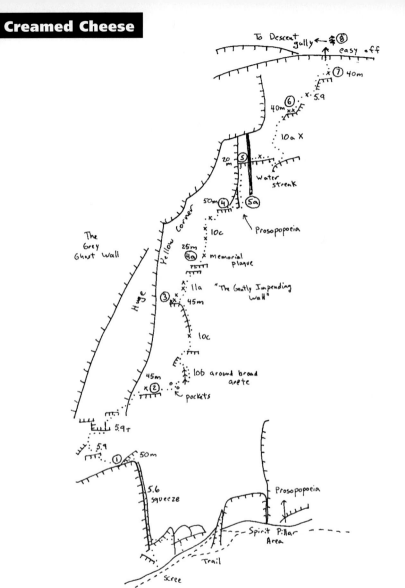

EPITAPH WALL

Creamed Cheese***   310 m, 11a   2-4 pins, small wires/RPs, cams to #3 Camalot

96

Creamed Cheese

2. 45 m, 5.9+ R. Move up left over some blocks to a small ledge. Climb a steep wall (5.9, runout) to a small left-facing corner and roof. Traverse right to a crack splitting the roof. Climb this (5.9+) to a short wall leading onto a good ledge. Traverse right to the main corner (runout), which is then climbed for 15 m to a good ledge on the right with a bolt belay.

3. 45 m, 5.10c R. Traverse right from the belay to some pockets (Friends or Tri-cams) near the edge of a broad arête. Climb the arête trending right to gain a short crack on the right-hand side. Climb this up and left to good holds then back right to a small ledge below a steep wall. Launch up the wall to a bolt (hidden from below) then continue to easier ground in a ramp leading up and left to a ledge with a piton and bolt belay.

4. 25 m, 5.11a. Climb the short but "the gently impending wall" above the belay past two bolts. There are, in fact three bolts, however, the first one is part of the belay. Above the second bolt there are several hard moves with ledge fall potential. The climbing quickly, however, gets much easier and leads up and right past several ledges to a single bolt belay below a steep brown wall. At this bolt there is a small plaque commemorating David Cheesmond.

5. 40 m, 5.10c. Climb the steep face past three bolts to a ledge system below the major roofs. Traverse right and make an awkward move into the large right-facing corner capped by an absolutely huge roof some 30 m above. Either belay here (pitons recommended) or if possible combine it with the following pitch.

6. 15 m, 5.7. Continue up the corner to a solid natural belay on a narrow ledge.

7. 40 m, 5.10a R. Traverse right on the ledge over the prominent water streak to a bolt. Continue right on the ledge to where it fades out. Step down and then climb across to a break that leads up to a good ledge. This is where the fun begins. Climb the unprotected but immaculate wall above on widely spaced holds. The line of least resistance seems to go up from the ledge, then trend left, then back right and up to an ill-defined corner. Follow the corner to a small, flat perch with a piton and bolt belay.

8. 40 m, 5.9. Climb up and right to a bolt. Continue up and right on excellent rock through corners and ledges until a single bad bolt on a good ledge 10 m below the top of the crag.

9. A short pitch of easy 5th class leads to the scree and eventually a tree belay. It is possible to combine pitches 8 and 9.

Prosopopoeia

EPITAPH WALL

Prosopopoeia**   310 m, 11b/c   gear to #4 Camalot, extra med. 3-4 pins

Prosopopoeia

**Prosopopoeia 310 m 5.11b/c
K. Haberl & S. Steiner, July 1995

"Prosopopoeia" is a fine route that was completed in a single day and in a bold style. The day was quite cold and scattered with rain showers and darkness. Between storms it took several efforts in the morning to establish the serious first pitch after which Keith Haberl and Shep Steiner "just somehow believed" that they would make the top. It is a committing route for the audacious "Hintersteiner Traverse" on pitch three cuts off any convenient means of escape. Except for pitch five, all the belays are off natural gear and are solid. Pins are not necessary but may be helpful for protection. It is recommended that the fixed piton belay on pitch five be replaced with bolts. "Prosopopoeia" is named in memory of Simon Parboosingh who was killed in an avalanche on Mount Athabasca and is Latin for "a voice from the grave."

"The perfect tip of the hat to the enthusiasm and energy we received on this day and others from the spirit of a great man."

The obvious feature of this route is the arching right-facing corner in the middle of the wall. After five-and-a-half pitches it joins "Creamed Cheese" at the large corner left of the prominent water streak and finishes as per that route. The rather exact gear descriptions are courtesy of Keith whose original, enthusiastic topo set some sort of record as it ran into four detailed pages.

Twenty metres right of the detached pillar there is an arching overhang just off the ground. The route starts up the crack that splits the left side of the roof (an angle piton is easily visible). There are numerous other cragging routes on either side of the route. See the Spirit Pillar topo starting on page 103 for details.

1. 25 m, 5.10+ R. Climb up and left to the crack through the roof to a "so-so" fixed angle piton (10d). Climb the crack and on to a slab and up to a no-hands rest and the only bolt on the route. Move left around a bulge and go up through a series of difficult "fins" that take "wires in between some of them, but everything flares, so it's all dubious." Continue up and right with increasing difficulty past a good fixed pin to a small ledge and a good natural belay below a right-facing corner.

2. 30 m, 5.10b. Climb the corner with great gear (10b) and eventually break onto the left arête (not steep) and a small stance below a blank wall. Continue up the unprotectable face on perfect rock (5.8) for 12 m to a natural belay around an enormous block on top of the Spirit Pillar formation.

3. 35 m, 5.11a. Move left from the belay past some loose blocks to a large flake with a fixed knifeblade. Continue left along the flake to a second knifeblade at the end of the flake. Back up the pin with a #4 Camalot "stuffed into an obtuse corner at the base of the overhanging wall kind of like it would if you were to try to cam it between your floor and the wall" and traverse left to make the committing Hintersteiner Traverse. This is a blind, dynamic launch leftwards to reach the edge of a left-facing corner. Continue up the corner (5.9) on immaculate rock (medium cams) to a slab and bomber natural stance "below the start of the big mofo yellow dihedral." Belay as far left as possible to avoid rock fall from the next pitch.

Prosopopoeia

4. 35 m, 5.11b/c. Climb the large right-facing corner with good nut protection to a loose, crumbling roof. This is "steep, strenuous and technical" but well protected with small to medium cams. Continue carefully past "the milk crate" on continuously steep and strenuous terrain. Scratch up to an excellent natural anchor and stance with nuts and medium cams.

5. 50 m, 5.10d. Climb up the exceptionally sustained corner "straying out onto the left wall where it seems like that would make easier climbing and back right into the corner for gear when you think you could get it." The corner ends with a short, very strenuous overhanging section that ends at an "airy and scary one-person perch" to the left. Belay off three fixed pitons and a "useless TCU."

6. 50 m, 5.9 R. Move left from the belay with the unprotected 5.9 crux coming in the first few moves. Continue on excellent rock up and slightly left aiming for the right-facing corner on pitch 6 of "Creamed Cheese." The only gear before the corner is a #1 TCU in a small slot about three-quarters of the way. The first ascentionists belayed on pitons on a ledge of "Creamed Cheese." It is recommended, however, to climb the "Creamed Cheese" corner (5.7) to a good natural belay (medium cams) at a small ledge.

7. 40 m, 5.10a R. Traverse right on the ledge over the prominent water streak to a bolt. Continue right on the ledge to where it fades out. Step down and then climb across to a break that leads up to a good ledge. This is where the fun begins. Climb the unprotected but immaculate wall above on widely spaced holds. The line of least resistance seems to go up from the ledge, then trend left, then back right and up to an ill-defined corner. Follow the corner to a small, flat perch with a piton and bolt belay.

8. 40 m, 5.9. Climb up and right to a bolt. Continue up and right on excellent rock through corners and ledges until a single bad bolt on a good ledge 10 m below the top of the crag.

9. A short pitch of easy 5th class leads to the scree and eventually a tree belay. It is possible to combine pitches 8 and 9.

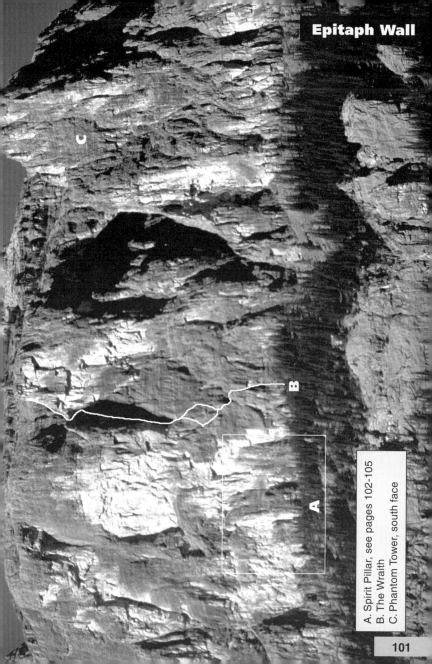

SPIRIT PILLAR

Between "Creamed Cheese" and "The Wraith" are several tongues of waterworn, grey rock between 20 and 50 metres high. This area is dominated by and named for a large left-facing corner of yellow rock that has been climbed by an unknown party at an unknown grade. There is a fixed piton about 25 m up the corner and on the FRA of "Maya" a piton was found at the top of the formation. The area is unique with a number of quality, pure-crack climbs with several at a moderate grade. Most of the activity to date has been on the natural lines although sport climbs have begun to make an appearance. All of the routes except "Spirit Pillar" and "Prosopopoeia" have bolt anchors but not all are chained and some may need slings replaced.

Dreefree 20 m, 5.10b
J. Josephson & L. Allison, 1994

Starting behind the detached pillar and right of an ugly chimney, this route wanders up some loose rock to a good but short finger crack and finishes through a roof to the top. From the anchor it is possible to top rope the steep arête to the left.

*Upspirits 18m, 5.9
F. Campbell, J. Josephson & S. Ritchie, Oct. 1993

A fun face climb in the middle of the feature that is a little runout through the easier middle section.

***Supernatural 18m, 5.10a
J. Josephson & T. Jones, June 1992

This is the obvious finger crack in the grey rock left of "Spirit Pillar" and is highly recommended. Finish at the "Up Spirits" belay.

Kobold Crack 20 m, 5.5 OW
B. Spear & M. Talbot, 1995

The first ascentionists, along with Joe Josephson, thought they'd scamper up this route simply as something to do at the end of a long day of cragging. Josephson got lucky when a ledge collapsed and he pitched over backwards only to have his one camming unit stop his head a mere metre from the ground. Needless to say, the others finished the route without him.

Spirit Pillar 50 m
Grade unknown
First ascent unknown. See history section in introduction.

This is perhaps the most obvious feature in the area. This large, left-facing corner of yellow rock looks steep and strenuous. It finishes through a series of overhangs near the second belay on "Prosopopoeia."

Spirit Pillar

SPIRIT PILLAR

- A Dreefree   10b   wires and cams to 1.5"
- B Upspirits*   9
- C Supernatural***   10a   wires and cams to 2"
- D Kobold Crack   5 OW
- E Spirit Pillar   Unknown

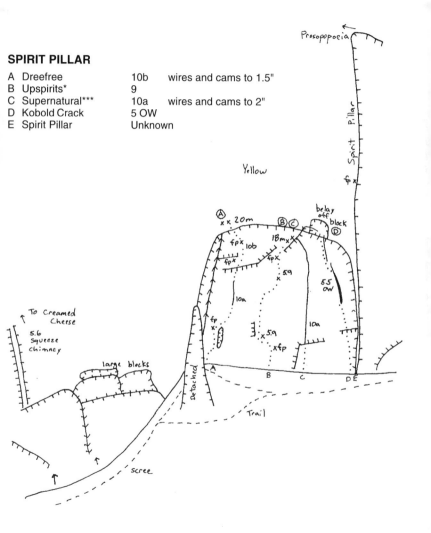

Spirit Pillar

**Prosopopoeia 310 m, 5.11b/c
See page 99 for more details.

**The Quabalah 26m, 5.10c
J. Josephson, June 1996

Prickly rock and a crux balance move characterizes this sport route. Stick clip the first bolt and finish at the chain belay on the first pitch of "Maya."

**Maya 50 m, pitch one, 5.7, pitch two, 5.9 OW
T. Jones & J. Josephson, June 1992

The first pitch is a classic moderate climb with good gear (wires and cams to 2.5 inches). The second pitch sees little traffic despite being quite good. A "Big Bro" or equivalent would be useful for protecting the initial wide crack. The crux pulls through a well-protected (#3 or 3.5 Friend) overhang near the top.

The Place of Dead Roads 30 m, 5.10a R
J. Josephson, 1995

This route branches right from halfway up pitch one of "Maya." Although it climbs a variety of interesting features the rock leaves something to be desired.

**Ghost Buster 20 m, 5.10b
J. Josephson & T. Jones, June 1992

This is a fine layback crack that was originally called "Dicky" because the gear at the crux can be awkward to arrange. It was changed later, however, to fit the "spirit" of the area.

*Poltergeist 20 m, 5.7
T. Jones & J. Josephson, June 1992

Climb the textured face on the left side of the corner past two bolts and into a shallow corner that leads to the same anchor as "Ghost Buster."

*Psychokinetic 20 m, 5.10a
T. Jones & J. Josephson, June 1992

This variation to "Poltergeist" takes a splitter, finger crack in the upper third. It is possible to contrive an almost independent line in the steep corner just right of "Poltergeist." Although it makes the route considerably harder you'd be forced to eliminate the desire to make an easy stem to the left.

Addam's Family 20 m, 5.6
S. Ritchie & J. Josephson, Oct. 1993

A right-facing corner/crack system named because the whole family can get up it.

Spirit Pillar

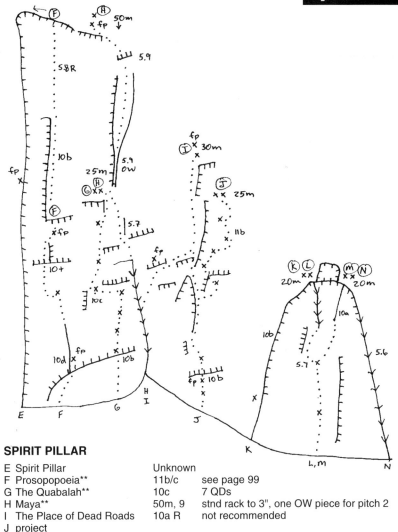

SPIRIT PILLAR

E	Spirit Pillar	Unknown
F	Prosopopoeia**	11b/c	see page 99
G	The Quabalah**	10c	7 QDs
H	Maya**	50m, 9	stnd rack to 3", one OW piece for pitch 2
I	The Place of Dead Roads	10a R	not recommended
J	project		
K	Ghost Buster**	10b	TCUs and cams to 2.5"
L	Poltergeist*	7	2-3 med size wires and cams
M	Psychokinetic*	10a	gear to 1.5"
N	Addam's Family	6	stnd rack

105

The Wraith

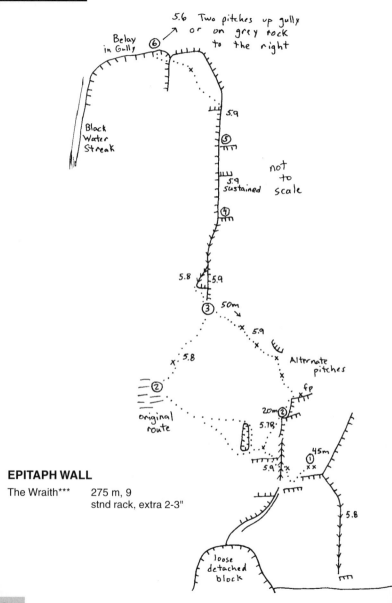

EPITAPH WALL

The Wraith***   275 m, 9
stnd rack, extra 2-3"

The Wraith

***The Wraith 275 m, 5.9
N. Hellewell & C. Perry, June 1977
Alternate pitches: T. Jones, E. Trouillot & J. Josephson, July 1992

Originally graded 5.8, a major variation was added to pitches two and three in 1992. As perhaps the most sustained 5.9 route in the area, it has since become a popular classic. The original line is somewhat easier but still highly recommended. When you pull the arête near the start of the second pitch, think about doing this without the bolt. A wild position indeed! The new variation above continues more or less straight up to the major corner and is similar to the crux pitch on Yamnuska's "Kahl Wall."

Ten metres to the right of "Addam's Family" there is a large detached block. Continue right for another 10 m to a prominent corner crack that begins on a ledge about 5 m off the ground. There is sometimes a small cairn at the base.

1. 45 m, 5.8. Climb loose rock to the ledge below the corner crack. Excellent climbing with good protection leads to a large ledge with a two-bolt belay.

2. 40 m, 5.9. Step down and traverse left and up to an arête and make a hard move up and round the corner and onto a ledge. Traverse left across a shallow scoop (bolt) and over a cracked pillar to good ledges. (Some parties have gone underneath the cracked pillar.) Continue up to the highest ledge at the base of a steeper section.

3. 40 m, 5.8+. Traverse right across the steep wall to a piton. Make a hard move up and continue up and right to a belay on a slab at the base of the prominent corner.

2. alt. 20 m, 5.9. Step down and traverse left and up to an arête and make a hard move up and round the corner and onto a ledge. Traverse left across a shallow scoop to a bolt. Climb up and back right on excellent rock (5.7 runout) to a corner. Climb the corner to a good ledge and belay off mid-sized camming units. With double ropes, this offers a good top rope for the second on the arête move.

3. alt. 50 m, 5.9. Climb the short corner above to a ledge (piton). Climb the steep face above up and left past four bolts to good ledge systems. Continue to a belay on a slab at the base of the prominent corner.

4. 45 m, 5.8. Above the belay, move left around a bulge or alternatively climb directly up the corner (5.9+). Follow the steep hand-crack to a large ledge in the corner.

5. 45 m, 5.9. Continue up the sustained corner past a roof to a ledge. Continue upwards to a smaller ledge below a blocky overhang. An incredible pitch!

6. 35 m, 5.8. Climb the overhang (it is not as hard as it looks) and into the corner above. Traverse up and left across the slab to a bolt. Continue left to a blocky corner. Make an awkward move over this and up into a surprising gully. Step over the edge and find a belay in a variety of blocks or against the opposite wall.

7. & 8. 80 m, 5.6. Easier climbing up the gully or on the grey rock to the right leads to the top.

The Wraith

Grant Statham on "The Wraith."
Photo: Dwayne Congdon.

108

PHANTOM TOWER

Phantom Tower defines the corner between the south-facing West Phantom Crag and the east-facing South Phantom Crag. The tower will be described in two parts; the South Face and the East Face.

Phantom Tower - South Face

A. Southwest Ridge
B. Phantom Cracks
C. South Face route

109

Phantom Tower - South Face

This face is located on the far east (right) side of the West Phantom Crag massif. It is separated from Epitaph Wall by a deep, ugly-looking chimney. The tower itself is an attractive form begging to be climbed. It does, however, suffer from rock that is more broken than the well-worn faces of its neighbours to the west.

Approach
Approach as for West Phantom Crag, see page 59 for details. Hike up to the base of the cliff below Grey Ghost Wall and follow a faint trail right (east) past Grey Ghost Wall and Epitaph Wall to a major scree gully draining the cleft between the tower and Epitaph Wall. Cross the gully to below the south face in 45-60 minutes from the car.

Descent
The original South Face ascent party walked off to the northeast and descended as for South Phantom Crag. Since then, the Bonanza Descent Gully has been established and is the recommended way. See page 61 for details.

Southwest Ridge 325 m, 5.7
C. Perry & A. Sole, 1978

The climb follows the left ridge of the tower practically all the way and is loose in places and not sustained. If you enjoy climbing and life, this route is not recommended. Start at the loose corner on the right of the ridge and climb this moving left near the top. (A traverse to the edge at about half-height may be worthwhile to avoid the blocky upper section.) Once on the ridge, continue on its left side following the natural line. Higher up, traverse right and up to the large shoulder at about three-quarters height. Climb a short blocky section then traverse to a good crack on the right side of the ridge. Continue up this to the top.

*South Face 325 m, 5.8 or 5.9
T. Jones, A. Dunlop, C. Perry & M. White, May 1975
Alternate pitch 2: T. Jones & J. Josephson, 1992

This classic route was the second major climb done in the Ghost River area and marked the beginning of a rapid spate of development in the late seventies. On the first ascent, the team wasn't sure if the formation was detached from the main wall. Expecting a long climb with an epic descent, they carried full bivouac gear. Their climb was made in about seven hours and to their surprise the top is flat with a walk off to the descent gully.

The climb follows a prominent crack line in the centre of the face. The middle portions of route lack interest but the position on the crux overhang of pitch 8 makes it worthwhile. Also, the variation pitch 2 adds a fine corner crack. On pitch 5 there are several natural looking lines leading out left. More than one party has followed these to end up on the Southwest Ridge—not a great option but better than the entire ridge.

The route starts to the right of the upper face at a shattered corner leading to the base of a prominent open book. A few metres to the right is a large tree growing close to the cliff and about 30 m farther right is a chimney system leading up to broken ledges on the east face.

Phantom Tower - South Face

PHANTOM TOWER - SOUTH FACE

A Phantom Cracks*   see page 112
B South Face route*   325 m, 8 or 9 stnd rack, 3-4 pins

Phantom Tower - South Face

1. 30 m, 5.7. Climb the shattered corner moving right and up to a belay at the base of the open book.
2. 45 m, 5.6. Drop down and traverse left around the outside corner. Follow diagonal cracks up and left to the large central ledge.
2. alt. 45 m, 5.9. Continue up the open book on good rock to a belay (pitons required) on the left at a diagonal break. Move the belay by scrambling back left down the break to join the original route.
3. 45 m, 5.5. Move the belay over to the left and then climb a groove system up and left.
4. 30 m, 5.6. Continue following a diagonal line up and left to a ledge below steep grooves.
5. 20 m, 5.7. Climb the grooves and then move right to a slab below a wide corner/crack. Note that the natural line continues up and left to join the Southwest Ridge at the upper shoulder. Care is necessary in locating the proper corner/crack.
6. 40 m, 5.8. Climb the crack and continue up the chimney above until it steepens.
7. 30 m, 5.7. Go up and then move across right to an easier groove system that leads back left to a good ledge below the upper crack. Alternatively, continue directly up the groove (5.9) to the ledge.
8. 45 m, 5.8. Follow the crack that becomes progressively more difficult to an overhang (piton). Pull through the roof (crux), moving right at the top over ledges to the base of the final corner.
9. 40 m, 5.7. Climb the corner and belay well over the top.

Phantom Cracks

There are two short routes on Phantom Tower that can be included as part of the Devil's Gap cragging routine. Located left of the "South Face Route" is a section of grey rock. At the left end of this there is a deep cleft behind a small blocky pinnacle that leads to an obvious steep offwidth called "Borderline." At the top of the pinnacle on the right is a steep, yellow jam crack known as the "Boundary Value Problem." Both climbs are approached by a short 5.6 pitch up the cleft and end at a fixed rappel station. See photo on page 109.

*Boundary Value Problem 30 m, 5.10c
B. Durtler & T. Jones, Sept. 1991

Take a collection of small to medium Friends and wires for this fine finger crack.

Borderline 30 m, 5.10d top rope
Blow the dust off of all of yours and your friends wide gear for this challenging offwidth. It has yet to be lead and can be protected by "Big Bro's," extra-large camming units. It has one fixed bolt.

Phantom Tower - East Face

Despite being the home of the Ghost's very first rock climb and some fine-looking, waterworn rock, this feature is perhaps the most obscure venue recorded in this book. Following natural crack/chimney lines, they were among the earliest routes put up in the mid seventies and have been rarely climbed on since. These were done in an era when Yosemite was considered the Mecca so it was the striking crack lines that attracted the early Ghost River pioneers to this wall.

The East Face of Phantom Tower is considerably wider than its sister South Face. In fact, it doesn't look like a tower at all. It is bordered on the left by the rounded southeast buttress of the tower and some 200 m to the right by a very deep, north-facing cleft that separates the tower from South Phantom Crag. See photo on page 114.

Approach & Descent

There are two approaches and descents for the East Face of Phantom Tower.

The first option is via the standard West Phantom Crag approach, see page 59. This entails hiking past the Epitaph Wall, the South Face of Phantom Tower and continuing around the corner and up to the East Face. Because your car will be in Devil's Gap it is recommended you descend by walking west along the top of West Phantom Crag to the Bonanza Descent Gully, see page 61 for details.

The second option is to approach as for South Phantom Crag and then continue south past Montana Buttress to the East Face. See page 147 for details. If you come this way, you will need to return to your car at the old CMC campsite. Use the South Phantom Crag descent to the right (north) of Montana Buttress, see page 148.

The times for either approach are the same, about 75 minutes. The West Phantom Crag approach and descent are more established and have easier travelling both along the base of the cliffs and along the top. Therefore, it seems the preferred way although the South Phantom Crag option was used for most of the first ascents.

Texas Peapod 200 m 5.8

D. Vockeroth & P. Robbins, Aug. 1971

The route was named after its more diminutive British equivalent by Chris Perry and Alan Burgess after their second ascent in 1977. Thinking they were on a new route, they found an old soft-metal piton on the last pitch. It was nearly 20 years later before Chris discovered Don Vockeroth as the culprit.

This route is roughly in the middle of the East Face and is easily distinguished as a deep, pod-shaped chimney that closes near the top. It is the farthest left of the obvious cracks that split the face.

Start directly below the line at the righthand of two short chimneys. Several pitches of easy climbing lead to a steep section below the upper chimney. Climb the right wall (5.8) and belay in the chimney beneath the overhanging section. Two 5.8 pitches directly up the chimney lead to the top. Above the easier-angled lower section it is possible to exit to the right up a steep chimney/crack that faces south. This was climbed by the same first ascentionists at a similar grade but no detailed information is availble.

Phantom Tower - East Face

Groucher's Corner 190 m, 5.8
A. Sole & R. Nelson, June 1978

To the right of the "Texas Peapod" on the protruding front face are two chimneys. The left-hand one peters out after two pitches (on the left skyline when viewed from below). "Groucher's Corner" climbs this chimney and then exits up the right-hand side of a large bowl.

1. 40 m, 5.7. Climb the right-facing chimney to belay on a ledge below the right of two cracks.
2. 45 m, 5.8. Climb the loose crack above, trending left near the top leading to ledges.
3. 40 m, 5.7. Climb up 10 m then left to a loose corner. Climb this traversing left at the top and up to ledges.
4. 25 m, 5.8. Climb the solid 15 m corner on the right.
5. 40 m, 5.7. Continue up slabs to the top.

*Supercrack 190 m, 5.8
C. Perry & P. Morrow, Aug. 1975

This chimney, immediately right of "Groucher's Corner," goes up to a large stepped roof at just over one-half height and turns into a groove above. It is the most attractive of the crack lines when viewed from the Big Hill and may be the best route on the face.

Climb the chimney trending left where it steepens. Traverse back in above the steep section and "back and foot" up to a small belay below the stepped roof. Stem out right and climb over the final bulge to the crack above. Steep climbing leads to a belay about 15 m higher. Two easier pitches lead to the top.

*Double Trouble 210 m, 5.9
C. Perry & N. Hellewell, June 1976

This interesting climb begins up the right hand of two crack lines at the north end of the face. It starts well right of the previous climbs in a steep, right-facing corner some 25 m left of the gully marking the edge of the East Face. Scramble up to a ledge on the right.

1. 20 m, 5.7. Climb the crack at the left end of the ledge for a few metres then traverse diagonally left over blocks to the main corner. Follow this to a small ledge above.
2. 20 m, 5.9 Climb the steep left wall (hard) to gain the groove on the left. Follow this past a large overhang to a belay at the foot of a chimney.
3 & 4. 85 m, 5.8. Follow this chimney-crack system for two pitches past several 5.8 sections and traverse left to large ledges.
5 & 6. 85 m, 5.9. Climb the crack above (5.8) trending right past an overhang and up a steep wall (crux) to the top. A memorable pitch that is "forever etched in my mind," claims Chris.

PHANTOM BLUFFS

Below West Phantom Crag there is a shorter bluff (30-70 m high) that runs the entire length of cliff from Spectre Crag at the west end to the large block-like formation of "The Haystack" below Phantom Tower. Along with a few scattered crags to the east, this is collectively called Phantom Bluffs and is littered with rock climbs with a wide variety of styles and difficulties. Most of the development has been on the east end below Phantom Tower on either side of the park boundary.

Routes face every direction making it a prime spot to chase or escape the sun depending upon the weather. Five more areas: Wild West Wall, Kemp Shield, Bonanza Descent Gully, Spirit Pillar and Phantom Tower all have routes that complete the Devil's Gap cragging circuit. It is quite reasonable to climb on several of these formations in a given day.

Borderline Buttress, Super Heroes Tower, The Sugar Loaf (aka Short But Sweet) and The Haystack are located near the eastern end of the cliff in a complex series of formations known as the Border Bluffs (see photo on page 118). These are the most popular and easily recognizable features and will be described first. The topos included with the following descriptions were painstakingly created and supplied by Jon Jones and were first printed in the 1995 edition of *Sport Climbs in the Canadian Rockies*.

Kolbassa Wall is an independent formation located down and right of Phantom Tower (above and east of the Border Bluffs). It is recognizable by its bright yellow south face. Morning Glory Tower is the easternmost of several small formations that lies along the ridge line running east from Kolbassa Wall.

"Ju-Jube" is a lonely route that lies to the west of the waterfall called "Malignant Mushroom" and below the right edge of the Kemp Shield. Despite several forays to the right of the waterfall it is the only rock climb to date to the west of the West Phantom Crag approach trail.

Each area will be described in an west to east fashion starting with "Ju-Jube" and ending with Morning Glory Tower.

Ju-Jube

Ju-Jube

"Ju-Jube" is the only climb on the lower band of cliffs west of the main West Phantom Crag approach trail. It is located near a large, right-facing corner about 250 m west of the waterfall/seepage that forms the ice climb "Malignant Mushroom." The waterfall is in the lower part of the Bonanza Descent Gully drainage. When viewed from the park boundary, the right-facing corner is below and slightly to the right of the Kemp Shield. "Ju-Jube" climbs the wall immediately right of the large corner and finishes up a clean, left-facing corner/crack.

The crack pitch is excellent and makes the climb well worth the walk. This was put up in July 1982 and was Andy Genereux's first, first ascent. Considering the number of classics he has scored and the different venues he has opened up, this makes the route historically noteworthy. Back in those days there were little or no available updates on Ghost River climbing so "Ju-Jube" was the scene of several "first ascents."

Approach Details

No trail has been established to the base of "Ju-Jube" but the best approach seems to be via the creekbed that leads up to the "Malignant Mushroom" waterfall. From the park boundary, go west along the riverbed until directly below the drainage and then follow the creekbed up through fairly open trees until it begins to narrow and the hillsides steepen. At this point, climb the steep west bank and then go diagonally up left through an open pine forest to a scree slope that leads up to the base of the climb. A suggested day is to combine this route with climbs at the Kemp Shield or Wild West Wall.

If the river level is high and precludes getting to the "Malignant Mushroom" drainage, it is possible to follow the standard West Phantom Crag trail to the base of Phantom Bluffs and then traverse west along the base.

Descent

Rappel from the large tree at the top (50 m) or scramble down a diagonal break in the cliffs to the east. The break could also be used to access Kemp Shield via the "Ju-Jube" approach or as a more direct means of descent from the upper cliffs. However, no trail has been established and the break is difficult to find from above. It is located directly below the edge of the buttress left of "Bonanza" and runs down from east to west.

**Ju-Jube 55 m, 5.8

A. Genereux, R. Lanthier & W. Rennie, July 1982

Begin a few metres right of the large, right-facing corner, directly below the upper crack. Take small wires and gear to 3.5".

1. 35 m, 5.7. Climb the slabby wall following weaknesses to a ledge just left of the upper corner/crack. Move right to a bolt belay.
2. 20 m, 5.8. Climb the crack to a large tree at the top.

The "true" first ascent of "Ju-Jube."
Photo: Andy Genereux collection.

Border Bluffs

The highest concentration of short, "user-friendly" routes along with one of the quickest approaches make this the most developed and understandably most-often visited venue in the Ghost River area.

Border Bluffs were developed principally by Andy Genereux and Jon Jones and have everything from prickly slabs, open books and arêtes to overhanging jug hauls. The earliest routes were done in a bold, ground-up style and have slowly evolved into fully-equipped sport climbs. Some of the bold yet moderate climbs of the early years have been retrofitted to make them more accessible to climbers who'se leading potential is at the stated grade. Others have been intentionally left in their original state to reflect the ethic of a lost era. The end result is a great crag with a little of something for everyone.

Approach

Leave your car at the Banff Park boundary. See page 36 for details to this point.

The standard approach to the bluffs is independent of and lies to the right (east) of the popular West Phantom Crag trail. This is the quickest way of reaching the Border Bluffs and can also be used for Kolbassa Wall and Morning Glory Tower. The trail begins on the north bank of the river about 250 m upstream from the park boundary at a shallow gully on the west side of a prominent aspen grove. The aspen grove is set at the base of a rounded hill that forms an open ridge higher up. At present, the trail is not well defined and more marker cairns are required. See photos on pages 59 and 136.

Wade the river and climb a steep bank to reach the base of the faint gully. Follow a game trail just left of the aspen grove for about five minutes to where the aspens begin to thin out on the right and then traverse up and right across the hillside to the open ridge. Continue up and left along the ridge following a trail and then head directly up over a rounded, semi-wooded bench (cairn). Continue over a smaller bench to a third larger bench. Once on top of this (good view of the Border Bluffs, some 300 m away) trend left across a flat area to more open ground and climb a scree slope with a small gully on its right side. This "trail" reaches Border Bluffs near the right side of Borderline Buttress.

Border Bluffs

Borderline Buttress

This crag is the farthest left of the established Border Bluffs. It faces due south and is characterized by steep slab climbing on excellent grey rock. The area was originally a challenging ground-up venue but recent drilling has produced some sport routes and retrofitted a few of the older climbs.

Borderline Buttress extends left from where the park boundary intersects the cliff (prominent cut line on the hillside below) to a vertical break and well-defined edge, beyond which the cliffs become more broken and less interesting. Most of the climbs end at a long, treed break at about two-thirds height and descent is by rappel. A prominent feature near the left end of the cliff is a long overlap about 12 m above the base.

Travellin' Light 45 m, 5.10b
D. Morgan & B. Huseby, June 1984

This early Dave Morgan route is characteristically runout. The original climb exited left as shown on the topo and the finishing pitch, which is also runout, was added later by A. Genereux, J. Jones and W. Rennie in 1985.

**Achilles 20 m, 5.10b
J. Jones, W. Rennie & A. Genereux, Aug. 1985

This route climbs a small pillar to the left of the overlap and was established ground-up. The crux section is sustained and the climb originally was a bold lead but has since been retrofitted. It ends about halfway up to the break at a fixed rappel station.

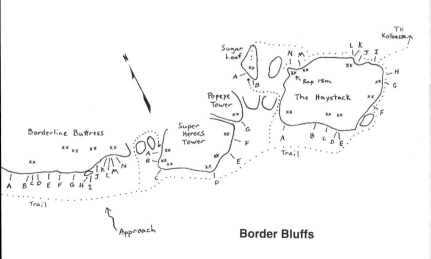

Border Bluffs

Borderline Buttress

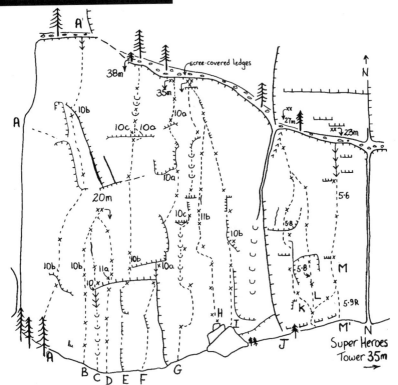

BORDERLINE BUTTRESS

A	Travellin' Light, original	10b R	wires
A'	Travellin' Light, direct	10b R	wires
B	Achilles**	10b	
C	Old Style*	10b	med wires
D	Stongbow*	11a	
E	On the Border***	10b R	wires
F	Revelations***	10a	wires
G	The Chimera***	10c R	wires, TCUs
H	Diawl**	11b	
I	Rhydd*	10b	
J	Checkpoint	6	gear to 3.5"
K	Cathedral Steps**	8	
L	Tuesday Afternoon*	8	
M	Border Rat**	6	
M'	Border Rat original start	9 R	
N	Bandidos	75 m, 6	gear to 3.5"

Borderline Buttress

*Old Style 20 m, 5.10b
J. Jones, 1985

Climb a shallow depression to the left end of the overlap and continue up the wall above to the fixed station of "Achilles."

*Strongbow 20 m, 5.11a R
J. Jones, 1994

A modern, if not slightly squeezed, sport route that gives good technical climbing up to the station on "Achilles."

***On the Border 40 m, 5.10b R
A. Genereux & R. Lanthier, May 1984

This is one of the early ground-up routes that has since been retrofitted. It climbs through the middle of the overlap, past a bolt, up the face to a second overlap, to a shallow groove that leads to the top.

***Revelations 40 m, 5.10a
A. Genereux & W. Rennie, May 1984

This excellent route breaks through the right-hand end of the overlap. It was the first route to be climbed on this section of Phantom Bluffs and marked the beginning of a stage of rapid development. It was established ground-up and two bolts have since been added to the upper section, which was originally led in a spring snowstorm.

***The Chimera 40 m, 5.10c R
A. Genereux & J. Jones, May 1985

"The Chimera" is one of the finer routes on the Bluffs. The route begins on the right side of a small arête just to the right of "Revelations." It moves over left to gain a shallow groove and continues up past a second groove with widely spaced protection to anchors near the top.

**Diawl 40 m, 5.11b
J. Jones, 1994

An excellent sport route on the blank wall just right of "The Chimera" that provides a marked contrast to the "traditional" routes on either side.

*Rhydd 40 m, 5.10b
J. Jones & A. Genereux, Aug. 1987

The route begins as per "Diawl" at the top of a large shattered block and climbs through a lower bulge via an obvious, left-facing corner.

Borderline Buttress

Checkpoint 35 m, 5.6
R. Lanthier & M. Parr, May 1986

Climb the obvious gully/crack to a tree on the ledge above.

**Cathedral Steps 35 m, 5.8
J. Jones, July 1987

Traverse up and left to a bolt and then climb an intermittent crack. Hard moves lead past bolts to the top on excellent grey rock. A moderate sport route!

*Tuesday Afternoon 35 m, 5.8
J. Jones, 1994

Another moderate clip-up that offers a right-handed variation to "Cathedral Steps."

**Border Rat 30 m, 5.6
A. Genereux & P. Farrar, Aug. 1990

This route, originally done with a 5.9 boulder start and given a gear list of "bolt, wires, TCUs and Friends to #2" has since been bolted and the start rerouted to be more consistent with the rest of the route. Start as for "Cathedral Steps" and climb up to the first bolt then move right and climb a shallow groove on good rock to a bolt belay.

Bandidos 75 m, 5.6
First ascent unknown—see historical section.

An unrecommended gear route that climbs an obvious gully/crack and continues above the lower section of the cliff.

Andy Genereux on the first ascent of
"Boy Wonder." Photo: Jon Jones.

SUPER HEROES TOWER

Despite its limited scope, the Super Heroes Tower offers some excellent climbing on three sides with the west and east faces being the best. The west face requires some tricky routefinding to gain a ledge part way up the tower. Climb an easy chimney between the tower and Borderline Buttress and traverse behind a small pinnacle and then down to reach the ledge. See the topo for a visual. The south and east faces are easily reached from the approach trail. The south face presents an impressive overhang just above the trail that is presently unclimbed.

Super Heroes Tower - West Face

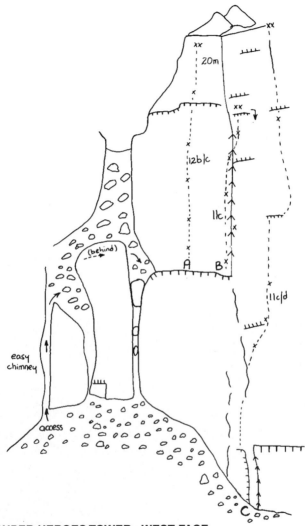

SUPER HEROES TOWER - WEST FACE

A Super Heroes Top Rope** 12b/c
B Boy Wonder*** 11c
C Batman Kicks Ass* 11c/d wires, Friends to #2.5

Super Heroes Tower - West Face

**Super Heroes Top Rope 20 m, 5.12b/c

Originally discovered by Andy Genereux in 1991, this is the eternal project. It was first bolted and climbed on top rope by Keith Pike of Colorado. Genereux later added two bolts and the chain anchor. The climbing is notoriously steep and technical with continuous 5.11+ climbing leading to a temperature-dependent, friction crux. Various attempts at a clean redpoint ascent have all failed.

***Boy Wonder 20 m, 5.11c
A. Genereux, Aug. 1991

Immortalized on the cover of the 1995 edition of *Sport Climbs in the Canadian Rockies*, this route takes the short yet classic arête right of "Super Heroes Top Rope."

*Batman Kicks Ass 30 m, 5.11c/d
A. Genereux & J. Jones

This route was originally graded 5.11b. After returning several years later and admitting to a bad memory for detail, Andy reluctantly upped the grade to represent the short but stiff crux moves. The route offers mostly 5.10 face and crack climbing with an out-of-context and devious crux.

Wanna Fly Like Superman

Bill Rennie climbing "Wanna Fly Like Superman." Photo: Andy Genereux.

Super Heroes Tower - East Face

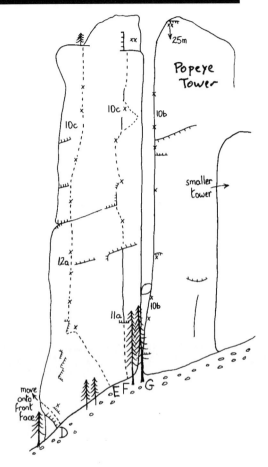

SUPER HEROES TOWER - EAST FACE & POPEYE TOWER

D Cling of the Spiderman**	10c	wires, Friends to #3, chain link hangers
E Superwoman's Wildest Dream***	12a	
F Wanna Fly Like Superman***	11a	wires, Friends to #2
G Popeye **	10b	QDs

Super Heroes Tower - East Face

**Cling of the Spiderman 30 m, 5.10c
A. Genereux, C. Yonge & S. Dougherty, 1989

Start on the east face of the tower and climb a rising traverse onto the south face and a bolt above the prominent overhang. Steep and sustained climbing with a hard crack to finish give this climb a bit of everything for the well-rounded climber. Yonge and Dougherty were in the right place at the right time to show up that day just as Andy had finished cleaning the route. Beware, the route has chain links for bolt hangers.

***Superwoman's Wildest Dream 30 m, 5.12a
A. Genereux & J. Jones, Aug. 1989

A sustained bottom section is reached by traversing left diagonally from the start of "Wanna Fly...." Continued hard climbing leads to pleasant 5.10 in the upper half.

***Wanna Fly Like Superman 25 m, 5.11a
A. Genereux, 1987

Andy was spurred on by Dave Morgan to attempt the free ascent of this line, which was originally a practice aid ladder established by Mike Blenkharn. It was clearly established that the route must be attempted from the ground up. Andy used wires over the rivets and arrived at the original station at two-thirds height a quivering mass (which is substantial). On rappel to clean the line, Andy popped all the rivets with his nut tool, which left an even sicker feeling in his stomach. The climb was rebolted and later extended to the top of the tower.

Popeye Tower

This somewhat independent tower lies immediately behind the east face of Super Heroes Tower and is home to one classic route.

**Popeye 25 m, 5.10b
J. Jones & R. Lanthier, 1987

"Popeye" climbs the slabby arête immediately north of the Super Heroes Tower. Originally a combo route with gear and bolts, it has suffered two separate retrofits, the latest one replacing the self-drives with Hilti bolts and a chain anchor.

The Sugar Loaf

Sometimes called the Short but Sweet Tower, this small feature is tucked in behind the Super Heroes Tower and The Haystack. To access the base of The Sugar Loaf scramble up a gully immediately left of the south face of The Haystack. It is possible to reach the top of the feature by walking around The Haystack to the north side. The wall is hard to see from this vantage and is not recommended on the first visit.

***Short but Sweet 25 m, 5.8
J. Jones & A. Genereux, June 1990

A sport route up the left side of the tower. It begins on a ledge below a corner (bolt).

**Sugar and Spice 30 m, 5.8
A. Genereux & C. Genereux, June 1990

A mixed gear (nuts) and bolted route on the face/arête on the right side of the tower.

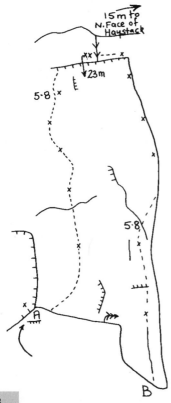

THE SUGAR LOAF

A Short but Sweet***	8	QDs
B Sugar and Spice**	8	wires

THE HAYSTACK

This aptly named feature is the right-most formation of the Border Bluffs. (There are a couple of small rock piles in the trees to the right but there are no significant cliffs until one reaches Morning Glory Spire, well to the east.) The Haystack is a large flat-topped block of rock that offers a wide variety of climbing. It has everything from the slabby south face to the steeper, scarier traditional routes of the east side, to the overhanging sport routes on the north face.

Descent
A number of the routes have their own anchors that can be used for rappelling. All others share a common descent anchor on the northwest corner above the route "Edge Clinger." This is a two-bolt, cabled anchor requiring 15 metres to reach the ground.

The second ascent of "Teenage Wasteland" via a new variation. Photo: Andy Genereux collection.

The Haystack - South Face

*Solitaire 40 m, 5.10b
A. Genereux, 1989

This route was established as an on-sight, roped solo using a dubious self belay system. Even with a proper belay the route still requires some traditional leading skills.

*The Grooves 40 m, 5.7
First ascent unknown. See history, starting page 21.

Start behind large trees and follow the shallow groove that angles up and left. At the top move left to the fixed anchor of "Solitaire."

*Midlife Crisis 40 m, 5.10d
J. Jones & A. Genereux, Aug. 1989

Hard moves surmount a steep face that leads to pleasant climbing above on a faint rib. This leads to the anchor.

***Teenage Wasteland 70 m, 5.9 R
Original route: J. Marshall & partner(s), 1981
Variation: A. Genereux & J. Jones, 1990

This route starts at flat area behind trees at lowest part of crag. The crux is getting to the first bolt. Above the bolt the original line traversed right to a loose corner and climbed up to a single bolt anchor (as for "Waste of Time" on topo). The route then went up and left to a bolt (now a two-bolt station) on a small pedestal. Above here the route went up a short distance and then left across a slab into a right-facing corner (marked on topo).

The variation was added on lead and is now the preferred and highly recommended route. From the first bolt continue straight up to the two-bolt anchor at the pedestal. The second pitch goes up and then left to follow good rock past two bolts right of the original corner.

**Wasted 70 m, 5.10b
C. Yonge & A. Genereux, 1984

This direct finish to "Teenage Wasteland" follows a shallow groove with a difficult overlap. Like the original route, this was first put up in traditional style with sketchy gear. The final piton has been replaced with a bolt and several small wire placements have been cleaned out to make this a better protected outing.

Waste of Time 70 m, 5.10b R
C. Yonge, S. Carr & J. Rollins, 1989

This meandering route climbs part of the original "Teenage Wasteland" and then heads up and right to the top of the tower.

The Haystack - South Face

***Lord of the Flies 45 m, 5.10d
J. Jones & A. Genereux, 1989

Start right of a detached pinnacle on the right side of the face. Some sustained climbing leads up to a series of overlaps (crux). Move right to gain a shallow corner to a bolt belay. This climb was once rather serious but has since been extensively retrofitted.

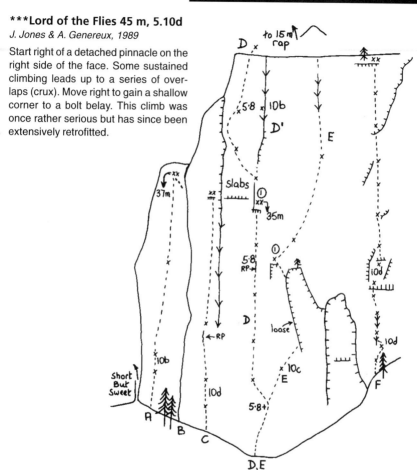

THE HAYSTACK, SOUTH FACE

A	Solitaire*	10b	wires, TCUs
B	The Grooves*	7	wires, Friends to #2.5
C	Midlife Crisis*	10d	wires, RPs
D	Teenage Wasteland***	70m, 9 R	wires, RPs, #2 Friend
D'	Wasted**	70m, 10b	wires
E	Waste of Time	70m, 10c R	wires
F	Lord of the Flies***	10d	QDs

The Haystack - East Face

*Little Bo-Peep 25 m, 5.10c
A. Genereux & J. Jones, 1991

This is the left hand of two routes on the east face. The climb was originally done to the top of the formation but it is now recommended to finish at the same anchor as "The Needle."

**The Needle 25 m, 5.11a
A. Genereux, 1988

Start with hard 5.10 climbing on natural gear in a shallow corner. After the corner peters out, hard moves past two bolts lead up to the belay.

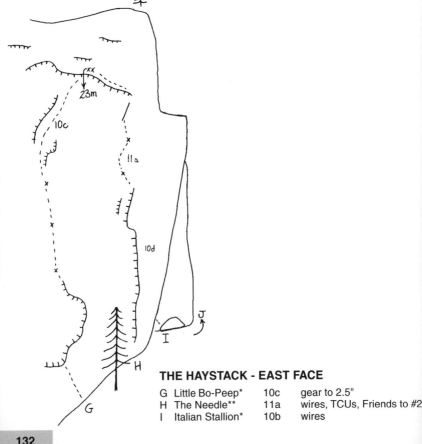

THE HAYSTACK - EAST FACE

G	Little Bo-Peep*	10c	gear to 2.5"
H	The Needle**	11a	wires, TCUs, Friends to #2
I	Italian Stallion*	10b	wires

The Haystack - North Face

*Italian Stallion 30 m, 5.10b
A. Genereux & R. Lanthier, 1987

This route was done on-sight in traditional style. Traverse left to below a fixed pin and make several hard moves past a second piton moving left to a pedestal. Several face moves lead past a bolt to a belay at a small tree.

***Imbroglio 30 m, 5.10d
A. Genereux & C. Yonge, 1984

"Imbroglio" is the first route on the imposing north face of The Haystack and remains one of the best. It was first done from the ground up using a couple of points of aid and then free climbed the following season. It follows an obvious and very steep groove line. Climb a runout but easy open book to bolts and the stem crux. Continue past fixed gear to a tree belay.

**Lethal Weapon 20 m, 5.12a
A. Genereux & J. Jones, July 1990

A pumpy, thin line right of "Imbroglio." Equipped with chain link hangers, this route and the next are in dire need of retrofitting with proper bolt hangers.

**Arms Race 20 m, 5.12a
A. Genereux & J. Jones, July 1990

This alternative finish to "Lethal Weapon" takes the overhangs on the right for an even more strenuous finish.

**Mental Physics 20 m, 5.10c
A. Genereux & J. Jones, June 1990

A fine route and a good warm-up for the nasties to the left. A cruxy reach move in the middle leads to a difficult corner at the top. Traverse to the top of "Edge Clinger" to descend.

***Edge Clinger 18m, 5.11b
A. Genereux, June 1990

A devious arête that marks the boundary of the north face and the even steeper yet unclimbed west face.

Hourglass

This abandoned project is marked by a single bolt with a homemade hanger a little ways right of "Edge Clinger" on the west face. It is named for the prominent feature low down on the route. "It's only matter of time before it disappears."

Edge Clinger

Doug Heinrich (climbing) and Russ Clune warming up on "Edge Clinger." Photo: Joe Josephson.

The Haystack - North Face

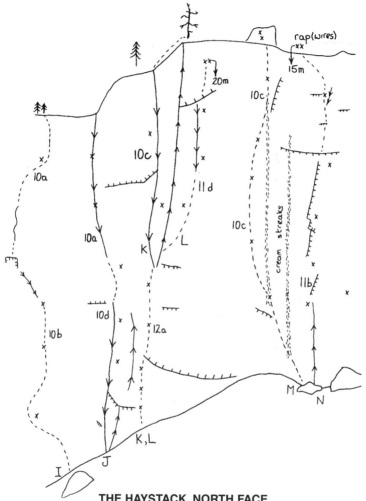

THE HAYSTACK, NORTH FACE

I	Italian Stallion*	10b	wires
J	Imbroglio***	10d	QDs
K	Lethal Weapon**	12a	chain link hangers
L	Arms Race**	12a	chain link hangers
M	Mental Physics**	10c	QDs
N	Edge Clinger***	11b	QDs

KOLBASSA WALL

Kolbassa Wall is situated immediately to the east of The Haystack and higher up the hillside. It is the largest of the cliffs in the lower tier and has three distinct faces. The most prominent of these is the South Face. The cliff then turns 90 degrees into an east-facing wall that extends over to a second, smaller and scruffier, south-facing wing. The cliff has received little attention until recently and seems long overdue for development.

Approach

Kolbassa Wall can be reached quite easily from The Haystack although presently no definite trail has been established. From the path below The Haystack, traverse right through fairly open trees, rising only slightly, until an open slope is reached and the South Face of Kolbassa Wall comes into view. Climb directly up the centre of the slope and then cut over to the crag near the top.

When going directly to the crag, the best approach is probably to follow the main West Phantom Crags trail to the base of the upper cliffs and then traverse right beneath Phantom Tower to reach the top of the cliff at its west end.

Kolbassa Wall Approach

A. Border Bluffs
B. Kolbassa Wall - South Face
C. Kolbassa Wall - East Bay

Kolbassa Wall - South Face

This part of the cliff consists of predominantly yellow rock and is split, towards its left end, by several prominent crack lines. All the climbs completed to date were done in one day by a group of motivated youth. The climbs are gear routes and are described briefly below and shown in the accompanying topo. There remains large expanses of steep, small-featured terrain that have not been attempted.

*Big Ass 15 m, 5.8
D. Bartrom & B. Firth, July 1995

This route climbs a short and strenuous offwidth, set in a left-facing corner, at the extreme left end of the cliff. Big Bro's or equivalent are useful for protection.

*Allahu Akbar 35 m, 5.9
B. Firth & D. Bartrom, July 1995

"Allahu Akbar" begins just right of two large trees growing close to the face and starts up thin cracks to gain a prominent left-slanting ramp.

Ockham's Razor 40 m, 5.8
D. Bretslof & D. Crosley, July 1995

"Ockham's Razor" goes up the left side of a large block that forms an overhang near the ground and then follows a prominent wide crack to the top in one pitch.

**Yo' Mama 40 m, 5.10a
D. Crosley, D. Bretsloff, B. Firth & D. Bartrom, July 1995

Begin as for "Ockham's Razor" and above the initial block move down and make difficult moves across right to gain a right-trending break and corner system. The second pitch climbs up a striking hand crack and then up good corners to the top.

Kolbassa Wall

East Bay
A. If You Love Her, Buy Her A Gun
B. When You're This Big, They Call You Horse
C. The Freshest Sausages In the West

South Face
A. Allahu Akbar
B. Ockham's Razor
C. Yo' Mama

Kolbassa Wall

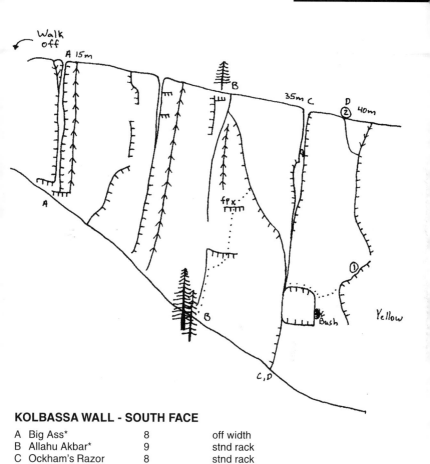

KOLBASSA WALL - SOUTH FACE

A	Big Ass*	8	off width
B	Allahu Akbar*	9	stnd rack
C	Ockham's Razor	8	stnd rack
D	Yo' Mama**	40 m, 10a	stnd rack

Kolbassa Wall - East Bay

To reach the East Bay walk downhill along the south face and turn the corner to the east face. A large block forming a squat pinnacle sits at the base near the edge. Walk through some trees and around the pinnacle to arrive at the East Bay, which is formed by the 50-60 m east face and a smaller, perpendicular wing that runs downhill and south toward Morning Glory Tower.

To date, three quality routes have been done in the East Bay although there is at least one project and a number of scrappy crack lines awaiting the adventurous.

**If You Love Her, Buy Her A Gun 55 m, 5.11a
J. Fehrman & L. Rotter, Aug. 1996

This fine two-pitch route was raided by a couple of visiting Americans. The first 11a pitch is 25 m while the second pitch to the top goes at 5.9. Because the pitches are so different, the Yanks thought they could get away with giving each pitch a label and thus get their name in the book twice—sorry, hosers. But seriously, if you're not up to 5.11 you could rappel in and do only the top pitch. It would, however, be very difficult to find from above unless you scope it out previously from the bottom. The route is located in the good grey rock near the left edge of the east face and begins from the top of a large block that sits at the base.

*When You're This Big, They Call You Horse 55 m, 5.9
J. Josephson & D. Crosley, May 1997

If you enjoy steep, 5.8-5.9 corner cracks on Yamnuska, this is the route for you. "Mr. Big" takes the left hand of two closely set crack lines in the middle of the east face. Despite being a predominately off-width-sized crack, you need not do any off-width climbing nor do you need any particularly wide gear, although a #4 Camalot or equivalent nicely protects the exit. Four bolts and a fixed pin, a variety of face holds, stemming, thin cracks and lay backing make for a sustained and engaging route.

project
An anchor at the top of the wall and several directional bolts marks this project on the fine grey wall found right of the two prominent crack lines and left of the crack/chimney line that marks the right-hand edge of the true east face.

**The Freshest Sausages In the Valley 30 m, 5.11a
D. Crosley, May 1997

"Sausages" is sandwiched on the narrow, grey wall between the corner/crack at the back of the bay and a prominent left-facing corner on the south wing. Being somewhat underequipped, the first ascentionists came without enough bolt hangers and so the route was first led with knifeblades on the bolts. It has since been outfitted with proper hangers. Technical and sustained moves with a crux mantle move are enhanced with exciting, but safe, left-handed clips.

Kolbassa Wall - East Bay

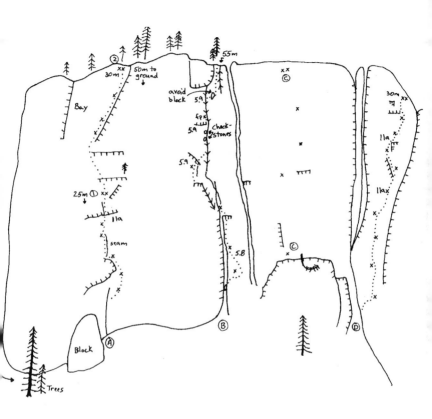

KOLBASSA WALL - EAST BAY

A If You Love Her, Buy Her A Gun**	55 m, 11a	cams and wires
B When Your'e This Big, They Call You Horse*	9	wires, TCUs, cams
C project		
D The Freshest Sausages In the Valley**	11a	9 QDs

MORNING GLORY TOWER

This small outcrop of steep grey rock faces east and has three short but interesting sport climbs. The crag itself is quite difficult to reach and tends to blend into the hillside from many viewpoints. When viewed from the south from the valley floor, it is situated down and east of Kolbassa Wall, beyond a broken south-facing crag, and appears only as a small, shattered pinnacle. Its clean, square-cut east face is best seen from the Big Hill. From here, it lies below and slightly east of the east face of Kolbassa Wall. See photo on page 60.

Approach

This crag would most likely be visited in combination with Border Bluffs or Kolbassa Wall. However, there is no established trail to the tower. From the trail below the Haystack at Border Bluffs, traverse across through fairly open trees as for Kolbassa Wall, but instead of climbing up, drop down slightly below a small, shattered crag consisting of two towers. Continue traversing across a treed slope for some distance to a shallow bowl in the hillside and then to open slopes beyond. There should now be a fairly large broken crag directly above and the backside of Morning Glory Tower should be visible below and farther east. This same point may be reached from Kolbassa Wall by descending a fairly open hillside below a band of broken crags that angles down to the east. The backside of Morning Glory Tower, however, is not easy to identify. From this direction, the cliff has a flat top, which blends into the hillside.

The three climbs are on the east face and are shown in the accompanying topo. They are all bolt protected face climbs on generally good rock. The short yet overwhelming south face of this tower is super steep and could perhaps be home to a truly hard sport project.

Yellow Jacket Special, project

Named for a hornet's nest that was painfully disturbed on the first foray to this formation.

**Early Morning Light 17 m, 5.10c

A. Genereux (roped—solo), 1994

Stick clip the first bolt.

**Rise and Shine 17m, 5.10a

A. Genereux (roped—solo), 1994

Stick clip the first bolt.

Morning Glory Tower

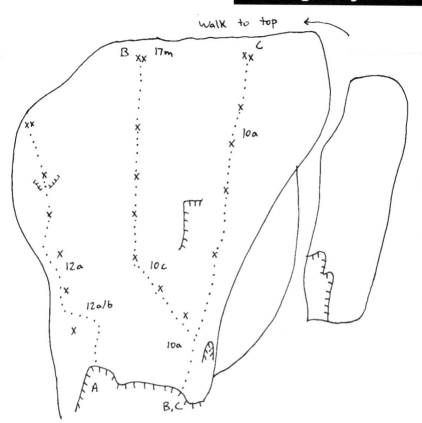

MORNING GLORY TOWER

A project
B Early Morning Light**   10c
C Rise and Shine**   10a

Ghost River Valley

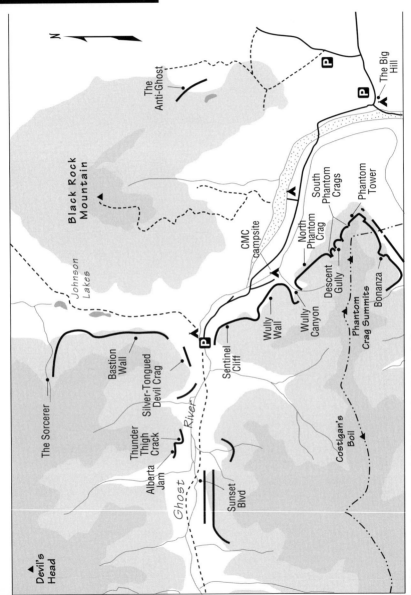

GHOST RIVER VALLEY

The Ghost River Valley lies at the bottom of the Big Hill and runs north-south perpendicular to the Minnewanka Valley and Devil's Gap. Way back when, the local utility company diverted the Ghost River so that it would flow west over a height of land (Devil's Gap) and enlarge Lake Minnewanka, which had been dammed to produce hydroelectric power. This is the main reason the access road to the Ghost exists. There are over four kilometres of east-facing cliffs rising above the diversion canals. They can be seen from the top of the Big Hill and extend out of sight to the right (north). Because of the diversion canal, which is very dangerous to cross at any time of the year, you must approach the cliffs from the bridge some 5 km north of the Big Hill.

The crags are, from south to north, the East Face of Phantom Tower (described under Devil's Gap, see page 113), South Phantom Crag, North Phantom Crag, Wully Canyon, Wully Wall and Sentinel Cliff. After Sentinel Cliff the Ghost River takes a 90 degree turn to the west and is then referred to as the "North Ghost." Overall, the Ghost Valley cliffs are shorter than the ones found in Devil's Gap and have a considerably shorter season owing to the eastern aspect. They have numerous outstanding features and were popular in the seventies and early eighties. More recent activity has begun to unearth some of the older climbs and opened up previously uncharted terrain, of which there is plenty.

CMC Campsite

Back in the mid to late seventies, when rock climbing in the Ghost was first being developed, the Calgary Mountain Club had a regular campsite below Wully Wall. This remains a fine area to camp and a good starting point for all the Ghost River Valley climbs except for Sentinel Cliff, which is reached by continuing north past the bridge for several kilometres. See the Sentinel Cliff section on page 182 for details.

Parking Access

From the bottom of the Big Hill, turn right and follow a good road north for about 1 km to a cable crossing. Somewhere before the cable, find a way left across the river to a good road on the other side. Once on the west bank, continue north past the "Black Rock Mountain" hiking trail sign to a small bridge over the diversion canal, 4.3 km from the Big Hill.

Just past the bridge turn sharply left on to a road paralleling the canal. If you are climbing on the "Consolation" area of Wully Wall, park after 200 m directly below the route. For Wully Canyon, North Phantom Crag or Montana Buttress drive another 200 m to where the road becomes impassable and the general area of the old CMC campsite.

SOUTH PHANTOM CRAG

South Phantom Crag is the section of cliff that extends from the East Face of Phantom Tower northward to a deep drainage separating it from The Streaker Wall on North Phantom Crag. South Phantom Crag consists of four very distinct buttresses or walls separated by deep gullies. They are identified from south to north (left to right) as South Phantom crags 1, 2, 3 and 4. To date, only buttress 3 has been climbed and is called Montana Buttress. The others await more creative names by those who manage to first climb them.

South Phantom Crag 1
This is the broad wall immediately right of the East Face of Phantom Tower. There is a series of grey water streaks pretty much in the middle of the face and this area looks to have the most potential. Right of the grey streaks, the wall holds large overhangs near the centre.

South Phantom Crag 2
This is the most buttress-like formation of the four. It is broken from Crag 1 on the left by a very steep and narrow slot. On the right edge, a much wider and larger drainage separates it from Montana Buttress.

Montana Buttress
A tower-like wall, Montana Buttress is one of the most impressive formations in the valley. It also has the most grey rock of any of the South Phantom crags. Subsequently, it appears to be the most climbable, although only the obvious line up the middle of the wall has been done.

South Phantom Crag 4
This wall is separated from Montana Buttress by the Descent Gully. It faces mostly north and is wider than it is tall. On its right end, it curves into a deep gully that separates South Phantom Crag from North Phantom Crag.

East Gully Approach
The most logical approach is from the CMC campsite although the cliffs could be also reached from Devil's Gap. See the Parking Access details for the CMC Campsite on page 145. From the CMC campsite, walk south along the gravel flats to the base of a major gully that splits the hillside below South and North Phantom crags (cairn). This is called "East Gully." The trail in the gully is presently not well-defined and is only marked intermittently by cairns. The version described below should become established with use. Follow the creekbed, which initially angles left (south), and then continue up an overgrown fire-fighting road on the left side. Rejoin the creekbed for a short distance and then continue up the old road again and follow it to its end where the cliff bands begin on the left side of the gully. Cross the creekbed and move up right to a trail on top of the north bank (cairn). Continue up fairly open slopes to the base of the burnt-out area and then angle up and left (cairns) through boulders and across scree to join the creekbed about 20 m below a huge boulder. Move up left around the boulder and either

South Phantom Descent Gully

diagonal up left to gain a good game trail that runs south below South Phantom Crag or continue up just left of the creekbed to reach the rock wall at the top of the gully. The former allows access to South Phantom Crag and the latter to The Streaker Wall and Vanishing Point on North Phantom Crag.

South Phantom Descent Gully

This along with the Bonanza Descent Gully are the major descent avenues for the Phantom Crags. Downclimb the gully (4th class) immediately north of Montana Buttress. See photo below and on page 146 and the map on page 144. This is the best descent for all climbs in the area including South Phantom Crag and the left side of North Phantom Crag. Unless you like rappel epics do not attempt to descend the next large gully (Upper East Gully) to the north between South Phantom Crag 4 and North Phantom Crag.

Care is required in locating the South Phantom Descent Gully from above, although some cairns are in place. The descent involves reasonable downclimbing if the easiest line is located.

From the base of the descent gully a good game trail leads over to the top of East Gully, which can be easily followed back down to the gravel flats. It is important not to descend too early because an obvious open slope that angles down toward East Gully ends in large cliff bands. Instead, continue north along the game trail until 150-200 m from the top of East Gully, then descend the open left side of a treed rib to the top of the large boulder with a good-sized tree growing above, move round the right side of this, drop down for about 20 m and then angle left across the bank following cairns. The remainder of the trail is the same as the East Gully approach.

South Phantom Descent Gully

148

MONTANA BUTTRESS

*Tough Trip Through Paradise 290 m, 5.10a/b
J. Josephson & B. Hendricks, July 1993

A good climb with interesting routefinding and in many places excellent rock. There are some moderately loose sections (pitches two and three) that should clean up with use and opportunities exist for several top-notch variations. The first ascent party completed the route in a day and well before darkness. They then, however, made the mistake of descending the wrong gully to the north of the normal descent. Half a rack and two chopped ropes later they made it back to the car by 1:00 a.m.

Gear: Small wires or RPs to Friend #3, three or four pitons, two hangers for 5/16" self-drive bolts (pitch five).

Begin about 40 m left of the edge of the Descent Gully at a right-slanting chimney system leading up to a group of small trees.

1. 50 m, 5.10a. Start in a clean left-facing corner just left of the right-slanting chimney system and after about 20 m, step left on to a clean slab. Traverse left below an overlap to its end and climb up thin flakes (knifeblades) until moves right can be made to a small ledge with a bolt. Climb a steep face above the bolt to a horizontal crack and then handrail left to a corner. Climb up a short distance to a ledge and belay below a loose bulge.

2. 55 m, 5.8. Climb over the bulge and continue up the corner to where it steepens. Step right and continue up a faint groove (runout) just right of the corner for 10 m until you can traverse across the corner above a roof. Climb up broken terrain to a ledge system and belay in a small corner.

3. 50 m, 5.8. Traverse left on the ledge system to a large corner. Climb up the corner on loose rock to a bolt, or alternatively climb clean rock to the right of the corner for about 10 m before stepping back into the corner. Climb steeply past a bolt toward a triangular, white overhang. Step right into a right-facing corner and climb up to a fixed belay on a slab below a large, white rock scar.

4. 45 m, 5.8 +. Climb up a steep corner past two fixed pins to a third pin below a large overhanging headwall. Traverse straight left on good grey rock past a bolt to a fixed pin. Step down and then go left to a semi-hanging belay in a shallow corner.

5. 50 m, 5.9+ or 10b. Climb a groove above the belay (runout) for 15 m. Traverse easily left under a large roof and across some blocks to a steep wall. Move up to a bolt (no hanger), climb straight up for 5 m (5.9+), then step left to a rest and a second bolt (no hanger). Alternatively, traverse left at the first bolt and climb steep flakes (5.10b) directly to the second bolt. From the second bolt, step up and then left into a short corner and climb it to a bolt/piton belay below a large roof.

6. 40 m, 5.7. Traverse left past a bolt to the edge of the overhang. Step down and traverse left into a corner system and climb up steep rock for 10 m. Step left again below a roof and onto easier ground. Follow it up to the first large tree.

7. Fourth class terrain traverses around the corner toward the back side of the buttress.

Montana Buttress

MONTANA BUTTRESS

A Tough Trip Through Paradise* 290 m, 10a/b see page 149
B Original Start* 100 m, 10a see page 151

From left to right: Dave Reid, Garry Jennings, Mike Sawyer,
Anda Rogan, Gerry Rogen, Jack Firth and Chris Perry. Photo: S. Climpson.

Montana Buttress

*Original Start 100 m, 5.10a
F. Campbell & R. Banard, 1990

This is the scene of several original attempts that stalled at the overhanging headwall on pitch 4. It begins about 30 m left of the previous route below a major groove system in the centre of the face. It joins "Tough Trip" at some treed ledges part way up the face and is likely to become the preferred way of doing the climb.

1. 35 m, 5.9. Climb up to a shallow groove and continue up this to a ledge on the right. Alternatively, climb an easier (5.7) line on the left moving across right higher up past a piton to join the main groove system.

2. 20 m, 5.10a. Continue up the groove past a bolt to an overhanging section. Go over this with difficulty to a bolt belay just above at a small ledge.

3. 45 m, 5.10a. Climb the groove above past a small, awkward overhang (bolt) and continue up to a large ledge with trees at the base of a right-facing corner system and the junction with "Tough Trip" near the beginning of pitch 3.

CMC Campsite, 1981

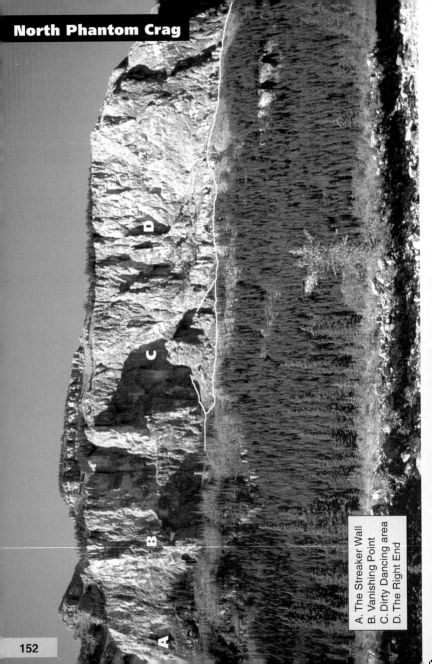

North Phantom Crag

A. The Streaker Wall
B. Vanishing Point
C. Dirty Dancing area
D. The Right End

152

Dirty Dancing

Looks like granite! Dave Crosley and Ben Firth attempting "Dirty Dancing." Photo: Paul Valiulis.

NORTH PHANTOM CRAG

An impressive cliff close to a kilometre long, North Phantom Crag is graced by 17 routes. Some are among the best in the Ghost, some have been totally forgotten, and some are among the worst. All the routes follow obvious natural features. It is the home of "Dirty Dancing," one of two top-down, multi-pitch sport routes established in the Ghost River area. The crag is somewhat disappointing for new route development but there are a few remaining natural lines of unknown quality and several areas of compact rock suitable for more modern styles of development. The crag's relatively moderate height, between 150 and 200 metres, and a walk to the top make this a likely scene for more routes using rappel tactics. As various approaches and descents are used, we have broken the wall into three parts: "The Streaker Wall," the unique "Vanishing Point" and the much wider "Right End," which includes everything north of the Vanishing Point.

The Streaker Wall

A. Haemorrhoid
B. The Streaker

The Streaker Wall

The left end of North Phantom Crag has a most bizarre history. Sometime in the 1960s there was a forest fire raging above and below the cliff. The Alberta Forest Service called in air support to drop fire retardant. Most of it, however, hit the cliff and permanently stained it red. The deep purple colour has started to fade over the years but the right hand of two prominent streaks can still be readily seen. Two appropriately named routes ascend The Streaker Wall.

Approach
The easiest approach is via the streambed known as the East Gully that is used for the South Phantom crags. See page 147 for details. Follow the trail up the gully to the base of the main cliff, cross to the north bank of the creekbed, and continue along a small trail immediately below The Streaker Wall. Expect about 40 minutes. The two climbs on the wall begin at the large treed ledge about 40 m above the trail, which is reached by scrambling up easy ground from the right.

Descent
For The Streaker Wall, it is recommended to use the descent gully for South Phantom Crag, see page 148.

Haemorrhoid 150 m, 5.11a
G. Powter & B. Wyvill, Sept. 1981

From the far left end of the large ledge, climb lower-angled slabs and a corner above for two pitches aiming for an obvious crack system that diagonals up and right. Once in the crack system, follow it to an obvious, left-facing exit corner that is climbed with difficulty and marginal protection to ledges at the top. Up to this corner the route maintains an average grade of 5.7. The exit corner, however, is very difficult and radically unprotected. Thus the reason for the route name, "The climb is bright red and a pain in the ass."

**The Streaker 145 m, 5.9 R
C. Perry, J. Firth & M. White, July 1975

From the approach, the line of "The Streaker" is obvious and quite striking. A lower crack system, which curves slightly to the left, connects via an undercut groove to a ledge in the centre of the face on the right. Above this, a large corner leads to the top. The first pitch is not well protected and overall, the route is quite difficult for its grade. However, the addition of a bolt runner and increased traffic could make the route a classic.

Begin at the right-hand end of the large ledge at the base of the lower crack, below and slightly left of the central ledge.

1. 35 m, 5.9 R. Follow the groove easily for about 6 m, then move left onto the wall. Climb this for about 8 m (runout—needs a bolt) until a rightward traverse leads back into the groove just above an overhang. Follow the groove to small ledges level with the only possible-looking traverse right.

North Phantom Crag

2. 5 m, 5.9. Traverse up and right across the steep wall to a small ledge just around the corner.
3. 30 m, 5.7+. Follow a groove exiting right and up to a tree on the central ledge.
4. 35 m, 5.7. Continue up corners to an alcove immediately below a perched block.
5. 40 m, 5.8. Step down and left, then climb up paralleling the main groove and rejoin it higher up. Move up over an awkward roof and continue up trending left at the top.

Vanishing Point/Right End

A. South Side
B. North Side
C. Whispering Smith
D. Moondance
E. Spooks

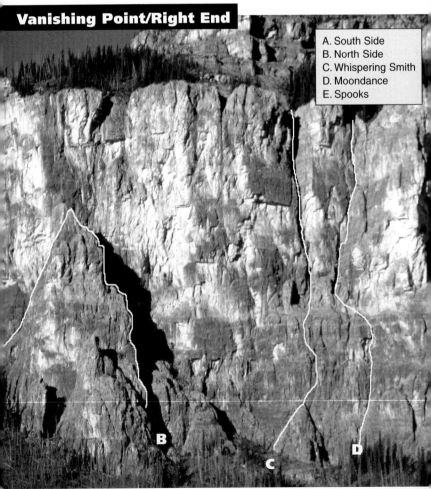

Vanishing Point

This is a large pinnacle, completely separated from the main face, that in certain light is impossible to see from the river flats. The top of the Point is about 100 m right of The Streaker Wall. See photos on opposite page and on page 152.

Approach Details
It takes about an hour to reach the Point from Wully Canyon. See page 159 for details. It can also be reached fairly easily from The Streaker Wall but no good trail has been established through the deadfall and new growth in the burnt-out area.

Descent
Scramble down from the top of the Point to rappel bolts at the top of pitch one of the South Side route. Rappel for 50 m, then scramble down the south gully.

South Side 55 m, 5.7
C. Perry & I. Staples, Aug. 1975

This is the better of the two routes up the pinnacle. Scramble up the gully on the south side to ledges on the right, about 10 m below the notch attaching the point to the main wall.
1. 45 m, 5.7. Traverse right onto the face and go up to a slabby ramp that diagonals up leftwards to the inside edge of the pinnacle. Follow this around on to the face overlooking the notch and climb up a groove to a small ledge with two rappel bolts about 10 m below the top of the pinnacle.
2. Scramble to the top.

North Side 85 m, 5.6
C. Perry & P. Morrow, July 1975

Beginning well to the right of the pinnacle, scramble up over easy ledges to gain the gully on its north side. Go up the gully until about 12 m below the notch and level with a slabby ledge that leads out left to ledges on the arête.
1. 25 m. Traverse to the arête.
2. 40 m. Diagonal up rightwards to an awkward right-facing corner. Climb this and continue more easily back up to the arête.
3. Scramble up to the top.

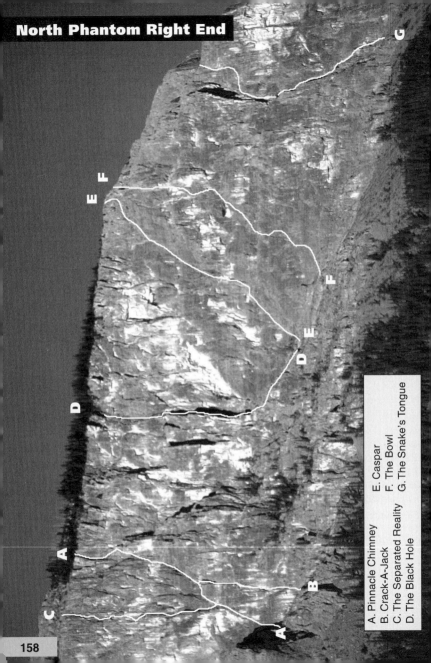

North Phantom Right End

A. Pinnacle Chimney
B. Crack-A-Jack
C. The Separated Reality
D. The Black Hole
E. Caspar
F. The Bowl
G. The Snake's Tongue

158

The Right End

The Right End is somewhat of a misnomer as it constitutes most of the cliff. The various sections are shown from left to right in photos on pages 156, 163 and 158. The quality of the rock varies widely from compact corners and prickly slabs to overhanging choss. In some places where the rock looks suspect the climbing is actually rather good (eg. "The Separated Reality"). Therefore we suggest you get out and explore, as the crag is a good bet for more than a few new routes.

Approach Details

It is best approached from the streambed to the north known as Wully Canyon. Park at the CMC campsite. See page 145 for details. At this point a washed-out road heads up the hill and into an old gravel pit. Walk across the pit and into the small stream coming from Wully Canyon. Continue up the canyon through a tiny gorge to where a trail on the left comes down the scree from the north end of the crag. Follow the trail up to a good path that leads back south across an open hillside and along the base of the crag. Enjoy—it is one of the easiest approaches in the Ghost. An easy 30 minutes will put you at the north end of the cliff.

The following is a quick rundown of the features that are encountered when traversing south along the base of the cliff. The climbs are then described from left to right in the normal fashion. After the path reaches the base of the cliff, it goes past a small cave and then passes below a black, overhanging chimney in the upper part of the face. This is the line of "Snake's Tongue," which avoids the upper chimney on the right. After rounding the corner, the pinnacle of "Vanishing Point" comes into view and the trail moves out to a small, rocky rib (cairns). The prominent overhang of "The Bowl" is now directly above and a scree slope leads up left to the base of "Caspar" and "The Black Hole." From the rib, the trail drops down left (cairns) under a small cliff and continues past a number of small cliffs and pinnacles to a broad scree gully that angles up left to "Crack-A-Jack" and "Pinnacle Chimney." If in doubt while crossing this section, stay low. Continuing left again (cairns) and staying low, the trail moves on to an open scree slope and becomes less distinct. At this point, it is probably best to continue traversing left, well below a large, square buttress at the base of the cliff, to the south side of a shallow scree gully below and left of the obvious diagonal break of "Spooks." A relatively firm scree slope then leads up right to the base of "Spooks" and the "Dirty Dancing" climbing area. To reach "Moondance," "Whispering Smith" and the north side of "Vanishing Point," climb the treed slope on the left and follow the base of the cliff southward. The bay of "Spooks" and "Dirty Dancing" can also be reached by thrashing directly up the scree slope immediately left of the square buttress (no trail at present).

Walk-Off Descent

For most routes, the quickest descent is to walk north into Wully Canyon. From the top of your climb, walk right and continue downhill until it starts getting very steep and cliffy. At this point, bear left and go into the creekbed running down from the East Phantom Crag Summit (aka Devil's Fang). Follow the stream down, easily passing the first small waterfall on the right. Above the second, larger waterfall cross over to the left (west) side of the creek and pick up a trail that descends easily into the main Wully Creek. Plan on 30-45 minutes depending upon which of the routes you're coming from.

The Right End

Rappel Descent

Only two full-length routes have fixed stations suitable for rappel. These are "Dirty Dancing" and "The Separated Reality." Either could be used but only "Dirty Dancing" may be considered suitably set up for mass use and is the only one possible with a single rope. However, it is tricky to locate from above for the first time. To use the "Dirty Dancing" rappel, traverse over to a depression forming a drainage in the scree slope above the route. About 10 m north of the drainage and 20 m above the main face there is a small cliff with a tree at the base. Rappel from the tree into the drainage (15 m) and locate fixed anchors in a second, small cliff at the top of the main face. Three 50 m rappels or six 25 m rappels from fixed stations lead to the base of the cliff—see the accompanying topo on page 164 and the photo on page 163. The anchors are fixed with rappel slings, not chains, and may need replacing.

Whispering Smith 170 m, 5.8

J. Firth, T. Jones & C. Perry, July 1975

Between "Vanishing Point" and the diagonal break of "Spooks" are two large, open book corners in the upper part of the face. "Whispering Smith" climbs the lefthand of these. See photo page 156. Of all the forgotten routes on the crag, this may be the most worth checking out. Take pitons.

Scramble up from the left to the top of a subsidiary buttress directly below the upper, prominent open book.

1. 35 m, 5.7. Traverse diagonally right across the wall, then up and a long way back left to a good ledge.
2. 35 m, 5.8. Climb the steep, shallow crack at the left end of the ledge and belay high on the ledges above.
3 & 4. 5.7+. Climb the corners above to the upper chimney and go up this belaying below a bulge just short of the top.
5. Move left over the bulge and continue up to the top.

Moondance 190 m, 5.8+

T. Jones & C. Perry, Sept. 1975

This interesting route, which may be closer to 5.9 in difficulty, follows the upper corner system to the right of "Whispering Smith." See photo page 156. It is named after an extremely long move right on the fifth pitch, which for a tall leader is "one small step" but for others may be a "giant leap." Begin about 10 m right of the subsidiary buttress of "Whispering Smith" at a small cave with a shattered yellow wall above. Take pitons.

1. 30 m, 5.8. Climb the wall to the right of the cave and make a hard move left to a shallow groove. Climb this to a ledge and continue up the easier groove above to a small belay ledge below a wide crack.
2. & 3. 40 m. Climb the crack and the chimney above to the large central ledges.
4. 30 m. Traverse left to a groove and climb this to the second of two ledges.

The Right End

5. 45 m, 5.8+. Climb the left-hand corner until it steepens (18 m), then make the "one small step" right to a ledge on the slab. Move right again round the corner and up the groove to a tree.

6. 45 m. A groove and chimney lead to the top.

Spooks 190 m, 5.7
J. Palmer & J. Carmichael, Sept. 1978

"Spooks" climbs a deep, right-facing chimney that diagonals up left through a more broken section in the middle of the cliff. See photo page 163. The route begins with a classic deep chimney (5.6) that is unprotected but probably more secure than it feels. Two long easy pitches lead to the upper section where the route moves out on to the left wall above a large chockstone. The next pitch gives enjoyable 5.7 climbing and a final 5.6 pitch leads to the top.

Ben Firth on the crux second pitch of "Dirty Dancing." Photo: Paul Valiulis.

The Right End

**More Dirty Dancing 25 m, 5.11c
A. Genereux (rap bolted & roped solo), Sept. 1995

Two sport routes have been established on the small buttress of excellent grey rock immediately left of the first pitch of "Spooks." Both climbs end at the fixed station at the beginning of the magnificent corner line of "Dirty Dancing." Details of the "Dirty Dancing" routes are given below and in the accompanying topo. See photo opposite.

The rock is good and the upper third of the pitch is very sustained to the final slab finish. This interesting climb could be used as a variation start to "Dirty Dancing." This would give five pitches of sustained 5.11 climbing—a must for those that would enjoy that many!

Another Dirty Dance
This very technical pitch, which has not been led at the time of publication, climbs the bolted arête on the left wall of the "Spooks" chimney.

***Dirty Dancing 145 m, 5.11d/12a
A. Genereux & J. Jones, Aug. 1991

This superb route is one of the best in the Ghost River Valley with sustained climbing, an incredible natural line and excellent rock. It follows a clean-cut, and very impressive, right-facing corner system directly above the first pitch of "Spooks." The first pitch, which is also the hardest, was climbed on-lead over several hours, but dirt deposited by drainage in the upper corner required cleaning from above. The remainder of the climb was then cleaned and bolted on rappel. Genereux gained access to the top by soloing "Spooks" with a 30 kilogram pack! He then went on to rappel, clean and hand-drill the route in a total of eight hours—an effort that helped inspire one of his nicknames, "The Human Hilti." Several 3/8" bolts were added on the first ascent to allow for 25 m rappels.

Gear: Friends to #4 with doubles of #2 and #2.5, a full set of TCUs and #4 to #7 Rocks for the first two pitches. Above this, wires and TCUs will suffice, so the rest of the gear can be left and retrieved on the descent. One 50 m rope is just long enough to rappel the route.

1. Ascend the chimney of "Spooks" for 25 m until above and behind two large chockstones. Traverse across the left wall of the chimney to a large patio ledge and bolt belay. Or alternatively, climb "Another Dirty Dance" or "More Dirty Dancing" directly to the patio belay bypassing the lower hanging anchor.

2. 25 m, 5.11d/12a. Step back across the chimney and onto the wall. Climb up to a small hole (large Friend) and then move right and up to a piton. Make hard moves left to a bolt. Sustained climbing past the next bolt leads to a small ledge. From here make difficult moves left to gain a shallow corner that is the start of the main open book. Hard, sustained climbing leads to a hanging belay.

Dirty Dancing area

A. Spooks
B. More Dirty Dancing
C. Dirty Dancing
D. Crack-A-Jack
E. The Separated Reality
F. Pinnacle Chimney

The Right End

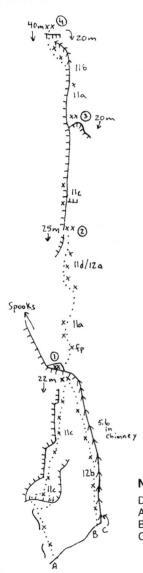
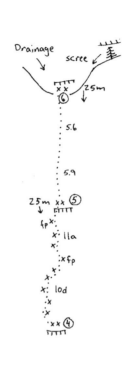

NORTH PHANTOM CRAG - DIRTY DANCING AREA

Dirty Dancing***   145 m, 11d/12a   see page 162
A More Dirty Dancing**   11c
B project
C Spooks   190m, 7   see page 161

The Right End

3. 25 m, 5.11c. Continue up the classic dihedral. Hard, sustained stemming past two bolts leads to a steep, finger/hand crack and more stemming up the corner to reach a pedestal ledge and bolt belay.

4. 20 m, 5.11b. Climb the corner above with continuously difficult moves. Below the roof move onto the left face to finish up to a large ledge and bolt belay.

5. 25 m, 5.11a. From the left side of the ledge make difficult moves up to a bolt. Continue up the face with sustained climbing on excellent grey rock. At the fourth bolt make an awkward move right to gain a ramp and shallow corner. Climb the corner moving onto the left wall at the top to a small ledge and bolt belay. This pitch is completely fixed and is the end of the major difficulties.

6. 25 m, 5.9. Climb the face directly above the stance past some wire placements to gain a slabby groove. Easier but runout climbing leads up to a bolt belay at the top.

Pinnacle Chimney 170 m, 5.6
J. Firth & T. Watson, 1976

"Pinnacle Chimney" is a right-slanting chimney that forms the left side of a wide, shallow pinnacle that is even more difficult to see than "Vanishing Point." The pinnacle is separated from the main face in its upper section and can be readily located from the trail by the obvious crack line of "Crack-A-Jack" on its left side. Photos pages 158 and 163, topo page 166.

1. 40 m. Follow the chimney on the left side of the pinnacle to below a difficult section.

2. 35 m. Continue past the fixed rappel point of "Crack-A-Jack" and up ledges to some small trees.

3. 20 m. Scramble up behind the pinnacle to its top.

4. 40 m. Traverse up diagonally leftwards across the face above the pinnacle to a ledge.

5. 35 m. Climb a short wall then go up and left to the top.

The Right End

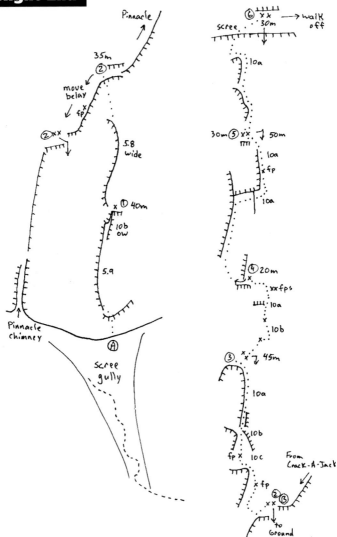

NORTH PHANTOM CRAG

A Crack-A-Jack***   75 m, 10b   stnd rack to #5 Camalot
B The Separated Reality**   230 m, 10c   stnd rack

The Right End

***Crack-A-Jack 75 m, 5.10b
J. Firth, J. Horne & M. Sawyer, 1976

This excellent crack climb, which was originally called a 5.9 hand crack, follows an obvious line leading to the left shoulder of the pinnacle.

1. 40 m, 5.10b. Follow the crack with increasing difficulty past an awkward off-width section through an overhang to a ledge with a single bolt.
2. 35 m, 5.8. Continue up the crack to ledges in the Pinnacle Chimney.
3. Down-climb the chimney to the left easily for 10 m to a fixed rappel point just above the first belay of "Pinnacle Chimney." Or, from this station continue to the top of the cliff via "The Separated Reality."

**The Separated Reality 230 m, 5.10c
B. Wyvill & T. Jones, June 1990

A well-protected, sustained climb on good rock throughout. When combined with "Crack-A-Jack" this route constitutes an exacting and enjoyable outing. The route name makes no illusions to the famous Yosemite test piece but rather suggests marital problems being suffered at the time. Take a standard rack, pitons not required.

It is possible to rappel the route with double ropes from fixed anchors (no chains) atop pitches 6, 5, 3 and the final rappel from the "Crack-A-Jack" station in "Pinnacle Chimney."

1. & 2. 80 m. As for "Crack-A-Jack," descend to the bolts at the rappel station.

1. alt. Climb the first pitch of "Pinnacle Chimney" to the fixed station.

3. 50 m, 5.10b. Traverse left and climb the ever-steepening groove (piton) until the crack closes (piton). Some interesting moves lead to a wider crack that is followed to a crevasse stance and a traditional belay.
4. 25 m, 5.10a. Step right (two bolts—rappel station), go right again around the arête and climb up to a bolt. Climb up and step back left and turn a small overhang on the right. Climb up easier ground to several pitons. Traverse left above to a good stance in a corner with a good wire and bolt belay.
5. 30 m, 5.10a. Traverse left and climb the groove to where it steepens unreasonably. Make a delicate traverse right under an overhang to reach a more accommodating groove (piton). Follow this to an exposed ledge on the left with a two-bolt belay.
6. 35 m, 5.10a. Continue up the steep groove to the top. There are two fixed pitons in a scruffy cliff some distance back from the edge.

The Black Hole 150 m, 5.7
N. Hellewell & C. Perry, June 1976

This forgettable route climbs a very unappealing chimney on the right side of a large pillar that leans against the face near the right end of the cliff. See photo page 158. It is situated opposite "Caspar" at the top of the scree slope, up and left of the small, rocky rib noted in the trail description. Scramble up the scree slope and continue up and left in a gully to the base of the chimney.

Crack-A-Jack

Mike Sawyer having the first "Crack-A-Jack," 1976. Photo: Chris Perry.

The Right End

1. 30 m. 5.7. Avoid the initial off-width section by climbing a cracked wall on the left and then hand traversing back right into the chimney (crux). Move up to a belay, deep inside the chimney.
2. 45 m. Climb a steep crack in the outer wall of the chimney to a ledge on the outside, near the top of the leaning buttress that forms the chimney.
3. 35 m. Move up on to the main face and continue up into the shallow groove above.
4. 40 m. Climb the groove to the top.

Caspar 160 m, 5.6
J. Firth & C. Perry, 1976

This route climbs the obvious diagonal chimney at the right end of the cliff. Photo page 158. It is probably the easiest climb in the Ghost and as such is a worthwhile beginner's route. The climbing is varied and the rock is reasonably solid. The route follows the wall to the right of the chimney for most of the way and exits to the right at the top.

The Bowl 165 m, 5.8+
J. Firth, J. Horne & M. Sawyer, June 1976.

On the buttress to the right of "Caspar" there is a large overhang at just over half height with a left-facing corner above and to its right. The overhang is directly above the small, rocky rib noted in the trail description. "The Bowl" climbs the face below and left of the overhang, traverses right below it and then follows the corner to the top. Some large gear (4 inches) is needed for the top crack, which is the crux. From the trail, scramble up to below and slightly left of the overhang and then follow easy ledges out for about 10 m on to the face.

1. 20 m. Move up and right, then go up past an awkward bulge to a ledge.
2. 35 m. Climb the wall on the left to a slab that trends up and right. At the top of the slab, traverse left past a block and go up to a higher ledge below and left of the large overhang.
3. 30 m. Traverse right on the ledge and climb an easy crack system leading past the right side of the overhang.
4. 35 m. Follow the crack until it steepens, about 6 m below a jammed block.
5. 45 m, 5.8+. Climb the crack, which is difficult at first (crux), to the top.

The Snake's Tongue 140 m, 5.6
O. Fluehler & J. Carmichael, 1978

"The Snake's Tongue" climbs the prominent crack system with a black overhanging chimney near the top at the north end of the cliff. Photo page 158. The upper chimney is avoided by traversing to a hidden crack on the right wall.

Follow the crack system for two pitches to a belay ledge on the left, about 6 m below an obvious fork in the chimney. Climb up to a good ledge, about 5 m higher, which leads out right for about 12 m to a flake crack. Climb this to the top.

WULLY CANYON

The Wully Canyon climbing area lies in the upper part of the streambed between North Phantom Crag and Wully Wall. It is home to a traditional route called "Rodents' Arête" and a couple more sport-oriented routes farther up the gorge. It is a pretty place with a relatively short approach. There is, unfortunately, a dearth of quality rock.

Approach

Park at the CMC campsite. See page 145 for details. At this point a washed-out road heads up the hill and into an old gravel pit. Walk across the pit and into the small stream coming from Wully Canyon. Continue up the canyon through a tiny gorge to where the canyon opens up. This is where the trail for North Phantom Crag takes off to the left. Upstream in the canyon there is a fork to the left that leads up (south) toward the Phantom Crag Summits. In the right-hand fork there is a short waterfall known as "Wully Falls." "Rodents' Arête" lies on the cliff above and to the right of the falls.

Descent

Perhaps the best descent from "Rodents' Arête" is to traverse far left and into the drainage above Wully Falls. Continue south, staying above the cliff bands and descend into the left-hand drainage coming down from the Phantom Crag Summits. Follow the stream down, easily passing the first small waterfall on the right. Above the second, larger waterfall cross over to the left (west) side of the creek and pick up a trail that descends easily into the main Wully Creek just below Wully Falls.

The other two climbs are situated in the canyon above Wully Falls and before a second waterfall. They are reached by following the streambed up to Wully Falls, climbing the scree slope on the north side, and then scramble left across the base of a buttress below "Rodents' Arête" and down into the upper gorge. "Womb With A View" climbs the right wall of the upper canyon starting below the second falls. A small buttress to the left of the second falls gives the line of "Priapism." The crack to the left of the buttress has also been climbed at 5.8. Above the second fall there is a narrow canyon and an interesting water spout. Note that the upper gorge is only in condition later in the year when the creek level is low.

Rodents' Arête 105 m, 5.6

A. Watts (Mouse) & C. Aspill (Rabbit), 1978

At the south end of Wully Wall the main cliff bends round to the west and parallels Wully Canyon. Near the west end of this section of south-facing cliff, directly above the waterfalls, is a prowlike buttress, the base of which forms the right side of the Wully Falls. This is the line of "Rodents' Arête."

The climb begins near the top of a scree slope to the right of the buttress. Despite its good line, the climb is reported to be quite scrappy.

1. 35 m. Traverse easily left across the buttress to a crack in a groove. Ascend this to a small stance.
2. 30 m. Climb up diagonally right onto the arête proper and go straight up on compact but slightly friable rock to a ledge.

3. 40 m. Traverse right for about 2 m and then go straight up the steep wall above to the top (not well protected).

Priapism 30 m, 5.10b
G. Powter, B. Wyvill, E. Trouillot & E. Niemy, July 1990

Climb the bulge and continue up the wall above to a fixed station (bolt protection).

*Womb With A View 40 m, 5.10c
B. Wyvill, G. Powter, E. Trouillot & E. Niemy, July 1990

Climb the wall (bolt runner) and arête to the right of the second waterfall and continue past a bolt runner until it is possible to swing left into a bottomless, bulge-capped groove (the Womb). Climb the Womb and exit diagonally left to where the route steepens. Climb the steep wall on the left (bolt runners) and exit left via an exciting mantle shelf move. The climbing is sustained and on good rock. Protection is partly on bolts but a selection of small nuts and two Friends (#3 and #4) is also required. It is recommended that an additional bolt be placed in the lower part of the climb where adequate protection is difficult to arrange.

Wully Wall

WULLY WALL

Wully Wall is a relatively large cliff situated immediately to the north of North Phantom Crag and separated from it by the deep drainage of Wully Canyon. Because of its proximity to the CMC campsite, the cliff received a fair amount of attention in the early years of Ghost River development. The name was given to the cliff by Bugs McKeith and reflects his professed affinity for sheep. In recent years Wully Wall has become a largely forgotten crag except for the route "Consolation," which is a popular, introductory route. However, "The Gateway" is a good climb with some interesting moves and "Big Willy" looks memorable, especially at its present, unchecked grade of 5.9. Recently, "Wully Sport" has been added as a harder (11b/c) and more direct version of "Wullywatchers." A small selection of pitons is required for most climbs except "Consolation" and "Wully Sport."

The most prominent feature on the cliff is a large, treed ledge referred to as Tree Island. It is situated toward the left side at about two-thirds height. At present five routes reach Tree Island directly and two separate finishes have been climbed. Two other full-length routes lie to the right of Tree Island. The rest of the routes on Wully Wall focus around the "Consolation" area.

Tree Island Approach
For all routes left of "Consolation" the best approach is via Wully Canyon at the south end of the cliff. Park at the CMC campsite. See page 145 for details. At this point a washed-out road heads up the hill and into an old gravel pit. Walk across the pit and into the small stream coming from Wully Canyon. Continue up the canyon through a tiny gorge to where the canyon opens up. Above this, either continue up the streambed to reach the Wully Canyon climbing area or climb easy slopes on the right to gain a small trail that runs up and then north along the base of Wully Wall.

Consolation Approach
To reach the "Consolation" area, turn left toward the CMC campsite and locate a small side road on the right, about 250 m south of the canal bridge, that leads to a small clearing in the trees (campsite). Starting from here, the easiest approach is via a small, overgrown gully that leads up to a scree cone immediately to the right of the route. The gully is difficult to find from below and is best located just before you pull into the side road. The gully lies about 75 m north of the parking campsite. A faint trail climbs its right bank and then moves over left near the top.

Tree Island Descent
If you climb a route to Tree Island and forego the top of the wall, it is possible to rappel "Jeff's Route" at the north end of Tree Island. Two 45 m ropes are required to reach easy ground in one rappel from a tree.

Scramble Descent (from the top of Wully Wall)
The normal descent is to the north although no good trail is yet established. One means of descent is to cut down the steep, wooded hillside immediately north of the cliff and follow a vague trail, flagged initially by intermittent seismic tape. However, the trail peters out lower

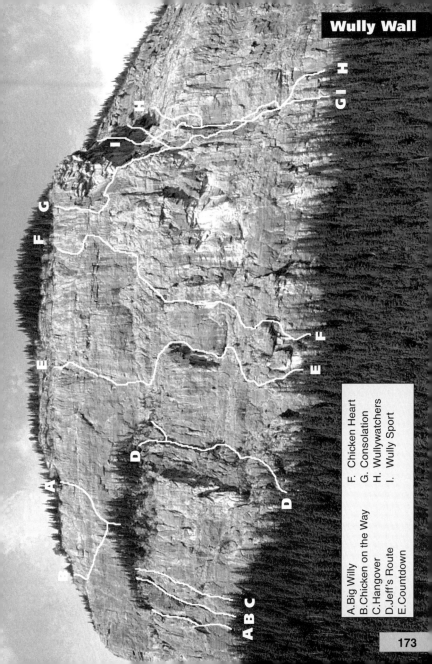

Wully Wall

down and a descent in this direction always seems to end in swinging off tree branches and down-climbing small cliffs. Probably the best descent route is to follow the top of the cliff some distance north and pick up a small game trail that leads to a major drainage. A large cliff near the top is bypassed by easy down-climbing on the right (south) and fairly open slopes then lead back to the road. The south end of the crag extends a long way back (west) beyond "Wully Canyon" and a descent in this direction is not recommended.

Rappel Descent (from the top of Wully Wall)

Recently, a rappel route has been established down the route "Wully Sport." See the topo on page 181. The top anchors are situated on the north side of the upper prow on a small cliff set back from the main face by a 2 to 3 m-wide gangway that slopes down slightly to the north. The anchors are about 60 m north from the top of "Consolation." Two 50 m ropes are required and the descent is recommended only for experienced climbers. The first rappel is very steep and descends to the base of the exit crack of "Wully Sport." Care is required in positioning the ropes on the next rappel, which goes down low-angled ground at first and then drops over the large overhang at the top of the open book corner of the "Wullywatchers." Two more 50 m rappels lead to the ground.

*The Gateway 105 m, 5.8+
C. Perry & M. White, 1978

When following the trail up from Wully Canyon to the base of the east-facing portion of the cliff, the most prominent feature is a wide corner with an impressive, and as yet unclimbed, crack on its left wall. Immediately right of this is a smaller, right-facing corner with a square-cut roof near its base. "The Gateway" climbs the corner and continues up to the south end of Tree Island. The second and third pitches are good and the grade of the route may be closer to 5.9.

1. 30 m. Climb a loose, easy pitch up from the left to the base of the crack.
2. 40 m, 5.8+. Layback the crack and go round the roof to a good foothold at the lip. Follow the crack more easily moving slightly right to the higher of two ledges.
3. 35 m. 5.8. Climb the chimney on the left bridging out left round the overhang and then following an easier crack system to Tree Island.

Big Willy 150 m, 5.9
B. McKeith & Alan Burgess, May 1978

Below the southernmost end of Tree Island are two deep corners. "Big Willy" climbs the left one, which begins halfway up the face at a large, right-facing overhang. Start left of the obvious, grassy groove of "Chicken on the Way."

Two short pitches left of the groove (5.6-5.7) lead to a belay 6 m below the roof. Traverse beneath the roof and layback the rib on the right to gain the groove above (5.9). Follow the crack to a belay on a large ledge. Scramble up to the highest point of Tree Island and climb the wall above for about 6 m to gain a fault line leading diagonally rightwards to the top.

Wully Wall

Chicken on the Way 150 m, 5.8
P. Morrow & W. Fritz, 1976

"Chicken on the Way" is named for a once-popular, if not slightly controversial, fast-food joint in Calgary. This route climbs the more obvious corner to the right of "Big Willy" and starts below the shallow, grassy groove. The groove begins at the highest point reached by the trail where it starts to drop down following the base of the cliff. Two pitches of good 5.7 climbing lead to the left end of Tree Island. Scramble up to the highest point as for "Big Willy." Climb the wall above for about 5 m and then make a long poorly protected diagonal traverse to a bay on the left (5.8, 45 m). From here a short, loose pitch leads to the top.

Hangover 150 m, 5.8
A. Sole & N. Hellewell, June 1978

Start a few metres right of "Chicken on the Way" below a left-facing crack.
1. Climb the crack, which ends after about 10 m. Avoid the steep, continuation crack by moving right for about 2 m to a corner that leads up to a tree belay.
2. Climb a crack on the right to a right-trending, yellow layback crack. Go around the roof to good jams above. Dynamic bridging leads up to Tree Island (surprisingly solid). Finish as for "Big Willy."

Jeff's Route 45 m, 5.7
J. Upton & E. Brooke, June 1976

"Jeff's Route" follows an obvious, right-facing corner leading to the right end of Tree Island. It can be used as a convenient means of descent by rappel. From the highest point on the trail below "Chicken on the Way," follow the trail down for about 65 m, and then scramble up and right to a large tree at the base of the corner. Climb the corner in one pitch, exiting either slightly to the left or by traversing right just before the top.

Countdown 195 m, 5.8
B. Keller & C. Perry, June 1978

This route climbs a prominent, right-facing corner that is level with, and about 60 m right of, "Jeff's Route." It continues directly up the slabby wall above to the top of the cliff. The slab on pitch 5 is poorly protected and the addition of one or two bolt runners is recommended. The name of the route was inspired by this pitch and refers to the depletion of Bruce Keller's "nine lives." Fortunately for Bruce, sport climbing was invented soon after this lead.

From the base of "Jeff's Route" follow the trail down to the cliff's lowest point and then continue around to a prominent right-facing corner formed by a huge block. Beginning about 12 m right of the corner, scramble up and right via an easy groove to a tree-covered ledge about 12 m above the ground. Belay immediately below two short corners, the right hand of which is capped by a small roof and has yellow rock on its right-hand wall.

Wully Wall

1. 20 m, 5.7. Traverse across yellow rock from the right to a shallow groove below the right-hand corner. Move up to a ledge and traverse left to the left-hand corner, which leads to more broken ground above.

2. 45 m. Scramble up rightwards to the base of the main corner.

3. 40 m, 5.7. Climb the corner to ledges on the left.

4. 15 m. Scramble up to a ledge below the upper wall and belay to the right of a steep slab below a small overlap. At the top of the slab there is an overhang with a crack on each side.

5. 35 m, 5.8. Traverse diagonally left onto the slab and go up to a small ledge on the left side. Climb up moving back right slightly and then go up to small ledges beneath the overhang (poorly protected). Continue via an awkward crack on the right side of the overhang.

6. 40 m. An easy crack system leads to the top.

Chicken Heart 230 m, 5.9 A1

A. Sole & N. Hellewell, June 1978

Immediately to the right of the corner of "Countdown," part way up the cliff, are three short grooves set close together. The route climbs the left-hand groove and then moves over to the right to exit near the final pitch of "Consolation."

Begin about 30 m to the right of "Countdown," at a short, cracked corner that leads up to broken ground.

1. 30 m, 5.8. Climb the corner and continue up past a tree to a second larger tree below and right of a right-facing corner. Move up and then across right to a yellow groove. Climb the groove and traverse right again to a ledge.

2. 45 m, 5.7. Climb the earthy groove on the right and then go diagonally rightwards to a tree beneath the left-hand groove noted above.

3. 45 m, 5.9, A1. Climb the groove, using one nut for aid, to ledges at the top.

4. 45 m, 5.6. Move up and across right to a chimney and climb this to a tree belay.

5. 45 m, 5.8. Move up for about 3 m and then go diagonally across to an easier groove, which is followed to beneath a steeper section near the top of the cliff.

6. 20 m, 5.6. Move left to a second corner and exit up this.

Paul Stoliker negotiates the traverse of "Consolation." Photo: Maria Bikaitis.

Consolation

Wully Wall

***Consolation 250 m, 5.7+
C. Perry & M. White, July 1977

Perhaps the outstanding feature of Wully Wall is the spectacular prow of overhanging rock in the upper portion of the middle of the cliff. The original line of "Consolation" follows a prominent, open book below and right of the prow and, in the finest of limestone traditions, traverses underneath it to exit up slabs on the left. To date, all of the climbing on this wall has centred around the first few pitches of this classic. As a result, there are numerous variations to any of the four routes in the area and over the years, a number of alternate pitches and belay options have been developed. The descriptions given below may differ slightly from the more recent preferences indicated on the topo.

The original "Consolation" route is remarkably sustained and has interesting climbing on almost every pitch. Approach via the gully, below and slightly to the right of the climb, as described in the introduction. Start about 10 m left of the top of the scree cone below the open book at a shallow groove leading to a ledge with a large tree. The groove has a bolt with an orange hanger about 10 m above the ground.

1. 35 m, 5.7. Climb the groove past an orange bolt and belay at the tree below a short right-facing corner.

2. 40 m, 5.7. Climb the corner and continue more easily to ledges at the foot of the open book. A belay can be taken here or after moving up and left into the main corner and then out to a ledge on the left wall by a small pinnacle.

2. alt. 40 m, 5.7. Move left over blocks for about 3 m and climb an easier corner up to the open book.

3. 45 m, 5.6. Move up into the open book and then go diagonally left across the wall past a blocky section until almost at a gully. Move up and back right to a small ledge with a flake. Either belay here or make awkward moves up and right to reach easier ground.

4. 15 m. Scramble up and belay below a lower band of overhangs.

5. 35 m, 5.7. Follow the slabs up and left beneath the overhangs past a piton to ledges that lead left round the edge of the buttress immediately below yellow roofs. Descend slightly to a bolt and nut belay.

4. & 5. alt. 5.7. From a piton belay by a small tree on the left at the top of pitch 3, move steeply left and climb a diagonal break up and left to reach the top of the fifth pitch.

6. 30 m, 5.7+. Climb up to a horizontal break in the slab and make a delicate foot traverse left to easier ground. Continue up and left to a small, exposed ledge. Either climb up a short distance and then traverse left around a steep arête to a ledge with a bolt belay or climb down a steep wall, across to a ledge and then up a groove to reach the same ledge (both equally difficult but the former is normally taken).

7. 35 m, 5.7+. Move up right with difficulty to regain the arête. Continue up a corner and then either move left slightly and climb a shallow groove or go directly up, past a piton and a small roof with a second piton, to the top.

Wully Wall

Direct Finish 5.8
T. Higgins, R. Hoare & M. White, 1979

This is hardly a direct finish as it simply traverses in the opposite direction from the normal route. The "Direct Finish" is somewhat more obvious than the normal route but was originally avoided because Chris wanted to add a few more pitches of "real" climbing. The true direct would be up the amazing prow that both routes conveniently avoid. From the top of pitch 4 (verbal description) on "Consolation," move up to the right and cross "Wully Sport" to a corner/crack system that trends up right to the top. A wide section higher up can be either climbed directly or by traversing onto the right wall for a few moves.

*Wullywatchers 150 m, 5.8
N. Hellewell & B. McKeith, May 1978

"Wullywatchers" is basically a variation on "Consolation," which begins just to the right of that route, climbs the same second pitch and then continues directly up the open book to exit up easy slabs on the right. The climb is reportedly worth doing for its third pitch up the open book.

1. 45 m, 5.7. Climb the right-facing corner at the top of an obvious scree cone about 10 m right of "Consolation." Move across left and up to the tree belay on that route.

2. 40 m, 5.7. Continue as for "Consolation," to the foot of the open book.

3. 35 m, 5.8. Climb a shallow, right-facing corner to the top of a small pillar in the open book (avoid the corner on the right that is loose). Move up right past a piton into the corner, and continue up with difficulty past an overhang (2 bolts) into the corner above. Ignore the fixed station of "Wully Sport" near the top of the open book 10 m above. Instead, traverse right to a ledge at the base of an exit groove.

4. 30 m, 5.6. Climb the groove that leads to easy slabs above. Scramble up to the top of the cliff.

**Wully Sport 205 m, 5.11b/c
A. Genereux & G. Rinke, Sept. 1995

"Wully Sport" is a harder and more direct version of "Wullywatchers" that finishes up a very impressive hand crack up the steep headwall above the main open-book corner. The route can also be used to descend by rappel as noted earlier and as marked in the accompanying topo.

Gear: Standard rack, multiples of #2-#2.5 Friends, several long slings.

1. 35 m, 5.8. Climb the first pitch of "Consolation" to the tree belay.

2. 20 m, 5.10c. Move right and up across the face to a bolt. Move right again and then make difficult moves up to gain a shallow seam. Climb this to a bolt belay at a small ledge. (Pitches 1 and 2 may be done as one 50 m lead.)

Wully Wall

3. 50 m, 5.9. Climb up and slightly left following several seams to gain the bottom of the open book of "Wullywatchers." The pitch may be split here. Continue as for "Wullywatchers" past the overhang and up to a fixed station below the large roof at the top of the open-book corner.

4. 50 m, 5.11a. Move right from the belay for about 3 m and climb up past two bolts on the right side of the overhang (short but strenuous) to gain a ledge above and on the left. Continue up a shallow corner above past a bolt and then wander up easy ground (crossing "Consolation Direct") for about 25 m to a bolt belay below the exit crack in the headwall.

5. 35 m, 5.11b/c. Traverse left for about 3 m and climb up past a left-facing corner and three bolts to a bay below an overhang. Move right under the overhang until it is possible to climb up past a bolt into a superb, curving crack in the headwall. Climb the crack with sustained moves for 25 m to a roof and then traverse right to a bolt belay. This great pitch offers full value for its grade.

6. 15 m, 5.10c. Continue up a shallow corner to a ledge and then climb a crack and layback flake to a bolt belay at the top.

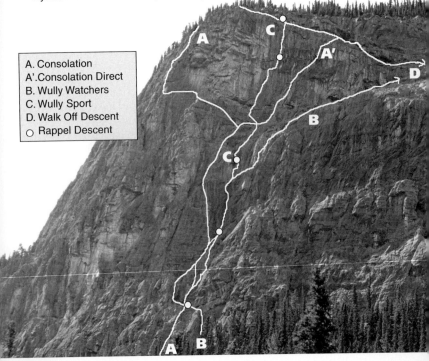

A. Consolation
A'. Consolation Direct
B. Wully Watchers
C. Wully Sport
D. Walk Off Descent
○ Rappel Descent

Wully Wall

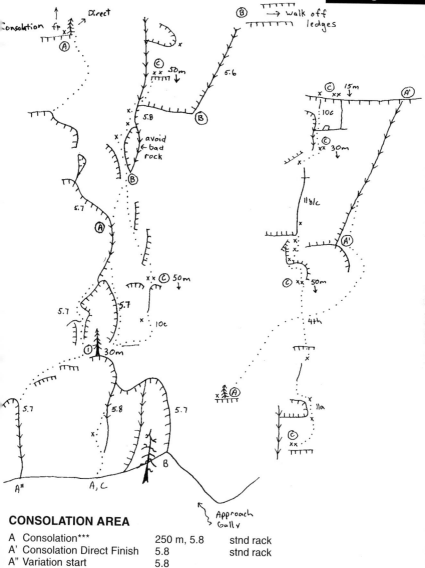

CONSOLATION AREA

A Consolation***	250 m, 5.8	stnd rack
A' Consolation Direct Finish	5.8	stnd rack
A" Variation start	5.8	
B The Wully Watchers	150 m, 5.8	stnd rack
C Wully Sport**	205 m, 11b/c	see page 179

181

SENTINEL CLIFF

This is the last cliff on the south (west) side of the valley before the river bends around to the west. The main cliff faces east, but the northern end of it rises virtually right out of the Ghost River where it makes the 90 degree turn. This north-facing section is very steep with large overhangs. The crag's namesake was an Inukshuk built by Bugs McKeith, which once stood at the base of the cliff. Considerably longer than it is tall, Sentinel Cliff has several pockets of excellent rock that have seen some development. The cliff is described in two sections: "Sentinel Bluffs," which is a pseudo-sport climbing area, and "Sentinel Crag." The obvious feature of the cliff is the large, open bay just left of centre. This is the home to the two-pitch crack known as "Cyclops" (5.10b), one of the best routes in the Ghost. Sentinel Bluffs lies below and about 200 m to the left.

Despite the existence of some modern sport climbs, there are several routes on Sentinel Bluffs from the early sport climbing era. Some of these routes have runouts on easier ground exceeding 10 metres!

Approach
Cross the diversion canal bridge near Wully Wall. Continue north along the main road through the trees until it opens up and a secondary road comes in from behind on the right (about 0.9 km from the bridge). The common approach for the entire cliff begins another 60 m past this road. Note: you may need to drive another 100-150 m to find a suitable parking area. Find an indistinct trail that heads uphill just to the left of a large scree slope that is hidden from the road by timber. About 30 minutes uphill should put you near the top of a scree cone on the right side of the Bluffs near the route "The Surprise."

Sentinel Cliff

SENTINEL BLUFFS

Sentinel Bluffs has many routes of a more moderate grade and the rock is above-average quality. The best routes are the face/friction climbs with the obvious breaks having the poorest rock. Gear recommendations are listed. Most of the routes were established from the ground-up, some with very little gear. Many of the bolts have homemade hangers and may require small profile carabiners to clip. It is a fine destination in itself or can easily be combined with one or more routes on Sentinel Crag to the right.

Descent
All of the Sentinel Bluff routes are descended via fixed anchors. Double ropes required.

Stretcher Case 50 m, 5.9 R
D. Morgan & T. Friesen, 1987

About halfway along the crag, somewhere to the left of the main Bluffs area, there is a right-facing corner with some bolt protection with aluminum hangers. Climb a face into the corner, then climb the corner and the runout face above to a belay. Not much more is known about the route.

*Minou 35 m, 5.10a
A. Skuce & A. Geoffry, 1987

"Minou" is a fun face-climbing route with the hard climbing well protected.

**Centrefold 25 m, 5.9/10a
A. Skuce & A. Geoffry, 1987

A very good route that starts in a short crack to gain the first two bolts and the climbing eases toward the belay.

*Pinup 30 m, 5.8
A. Skuce & A. Geoffry, 1986

This is a mixed-gear route that was rap bolted with natural gear placements left intact.

Black Mango 35 m, 5.8
A. Skuce & A. Geoffry, 1985

This route was done in order to access the top of the previous three routes. Climb the left-facing, shallow corner to a bolt belay to the right. Originally the route went left and continued toward the top of the crag—not recommended.

*Creeping Senility 35 m, 5.9
D. Morgan, D. Kemp & B. Huseby, 1986

This route was named by the late Dennis Kemp who was 60 at the time of the first ascent and thought the name appropriate.

Sentinel Bluffs

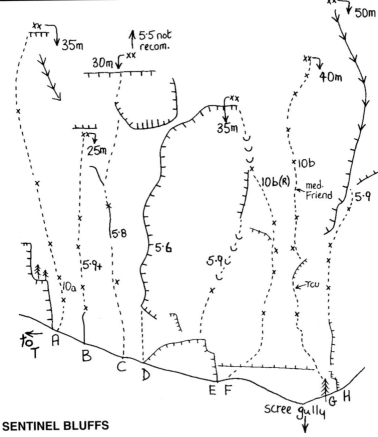

SENTINEL BLUFFS

A	Minou*	10a	
B	Centrefold**	9/10a	
C	Pinup*	8	wires, Friends, RPs
D	Black Mango	8	wires
E	Creeping Senility*	9	wires
F	Softly, Softly***	10b R	wires
G	Twinkle Toes***	10b	wires, TCUs, med Friend
H	Feeling Groovy*	9	wires, TCUs
T	Stretcher Case	9 R	unknown

Sentinel Bluffs

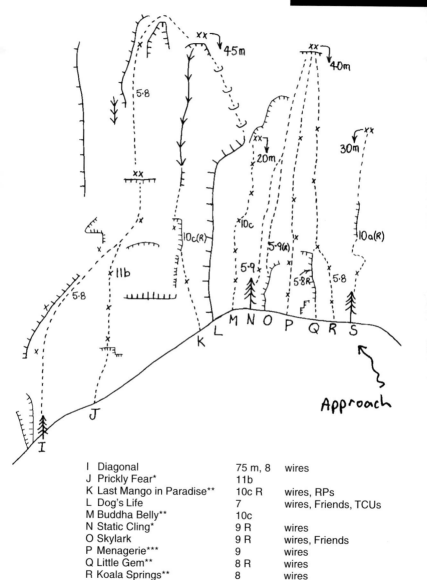

I Diagonal	75 m, 8	wires
J Prickly Fear*	11b	
K Last Mango in Paradise**	10c R	wires, RPs
L Dog's Life	7	wires, Friends, TCUs
M Buddha Belly**	10c	
N Static Cling*	9 R	wires
O Skylark	9 R	wires, Friends
P Menagerie***	9	wires
Q Little Gem**	8 R	wires
R Koala Springs**	8	wires
S The Surprise	10a R	wires

Sentinel Bluffs

***Softly Softly 35 m, 5.10b R
D. Morgan, 1986

This is an outstanding face climb that requires the leader to be steady at the stated grade.

***Twinkle Toes 40 m, 5.10b
A. Genereux & C. Genereux, 1990

"Twinkle Toes" offers excellent face climbing similar to "Softly, Softly." It was the first route in the area to be bolted on-sight, on-lead with a Hilti. As a result it has more reasonable protection than "Softly, Softly."

*Feeling Groovy 50 m, 5.9
D. Morgan & B. Huseby, 1985

This good climb with spacious gear climbs the corner just right of "Twinkle Toes."

Diagonal 75 m, 5.8
D. Morgan & B. Huseby, 1985

Pitch one follows an arch moving right over the steep headwall of "Prickly Fear." The second pitch is more run out on face climbing.

*Prickly Fear 30 m, 5.11b
D. Morgan & D. Kemp, 1986

Climb a short, steep headwall past three bolts to gain runout 5.8 ground. Most people don't bother with the second pitch of 5.8.

**Last Mango in Paradise 45 m, 5.10c R
D. Morgan & B. Huseby, 1985

This Morgan classic was done in the finest British fashion of meager gear on good rock. Face climb to a corner crack to finish.

Dog's Life 45 m, 5.7
D. Morgan & B. Huseby, 1985

This is a scrappy corner crack with some loose sections.

**Buddha Belly 20 m, 5.10c
A. Genereux & C. Genereux, 1990

"Buddha Belly" was done the same day as "Twinkle Toes" and also established from the ground up with the Hilti. It is a fun little face climb and the name describes the leader's "third lung."

Sentinel Bluffs

*Static Cling 40 m, 5.9 R
A. Skuce & D. Morgan, 1985

Climb the flake left of "Menagerie" to its top and make delicate moves out left to continue up the face. This route would be more fun with some protection; it is basically soloing at the stated grade with some protection for the crux sections.

Skylark 40 m, 5.9 R
D. Morgan (solo), 1985

Read the comments in the previous route description for an idea about the character of "Skylark." For the faint of heart, both routes can be top roped from the fixed station of "Menagerie."

***Menagerie 40 m, 5.9
D. Morgan, B. Huseby & A. Geoffry, 1985

This is one of the best routes at the Bluffs and fortunately it has decent protection. Climb the centre of the wall to the left of "Little Gem" to a bolt at 6 m. Steep climbing on big holds leads to a large scoop that is climbed to the belay of "Little Gem."

**Little Gem 40 m, 5.8 R
D. Morgan, 1985

Hard, unprotectable moves off the ground lead to a groove and a bolt some distance above. Climb the low-angled rib above to easier ground.

**Koala Springs 40 m, 5.8
I. Freeman, B. Huseby, A. Geoffry, 1985

This route was bolted on rappel by Dave Morgan and then led, on-sight, by the all-women's team of Isobel, Bev and Annick. It is a fun direct start to "Little Gem" that leads up a steep face past three bolts to the lower-angled face above.

The Surprise 30 m, 5.10a R
D. Morgan, 1985

This is one of the more serious routes at the Bluffs and to date may not be repeated. Climb to a bolt and then up left with difficulty into a corner. Easier climbing leads to a bolt belay left of the corner.

SENTINEL CRAG

Two hundred metres right of the Bluffs near the route "Déja-Vu," Sentinel Cliff takes a dramatic shift in steepness. As the cliff heads north it becomes steeper and has more well-defined features. It culminates in the large blocky overhangs on it's north face directly above the North Ghost parking area. This entire area right of the Bluffs is called Sentinel Crag. Only the area around the "Cyclops" bay has been explored even though the north end is easily the Ghost's most accessible rock.

Approach
Hike up to the base of the cliff as per the Bluffs area, see page 182 for details. Once at the cliff head right along the base. At this point you'll be headed down the right side of a scree cone. Go to the bottom of the cone and up and over another slightly larger scree cone. At the bottom of this second scree cone is a left-facing corner that is the start to "Déja-Vu."

The rest of the routes on the crag are accessed from the "Cyclops" bay. To reach the bay continue right past "Déja-Vu" up a steep slope to a short, scruffy cliff below the bay. Continue past the bay for 20-30 m until it is possible to easily scramble up to a large-ledge system below the route.

Descent
"Duveinafees" has its own rappel bolts while all other routes descend via "Cyclops." Some of the trees at the very edge of "Cyclops" are eroding away and are not suitable for anchors. There is a large, forked tree up and right of the bay that presents a fine anchor. Rappel 30 m to the fixed, piton belay on pitch one of "Cyclops." Another 40 m rappel leads to the ground.

Déja-Vu 135 m, 5.8
N. Hellewell, B. McKeith & D. Knaak, Sept. 1975

This follows a system of corners in the stepped buttress just left of "Cyclops." From the right end of the Sentinel Bluffs follow the crag to the right and go over the top of the next scree cone to an obvious large corner system.

1. 45 m, 5.6. Climb the open corner at the base of the buttress to a large ledge system. Scramble up and right to belay off the largest tree (20 cm diameter) directly below a steep hand crack.
2. 50 m, 5.7. About 5 m right of the steep crack follow a broken groove to a large ledge. From the ledge, climb up and right on a steep slab, over a small overhang (5.7) to easier ground and a small ledge. Traverse left to belay off a large tree.
3. 40 m, 5.8. Above the belay there is a flared corner with a snag hanging out over the top. Follow this to the top of the crag.

Make a somewhat exposed traverse right (45 m) through steep trees to the top of the "Cyclops" bay.

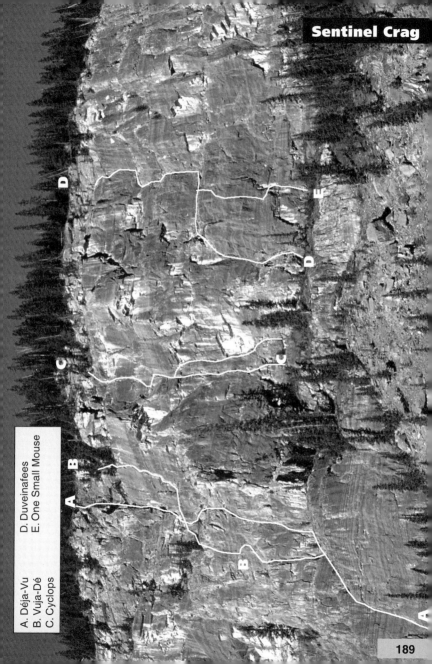

Sentinel Crag

*Vuja-Dé 140 m, 5.9
First ascent unknown.

This climb consists essentially of variations on pitches 2 and 3 of "Déja-Vu," which were established at various times in the last 15 years.

1. 45 m, 5.6. Climb the first pitch of "Déja-Vu."

2. 50 m, 5.9. From the tree climb the steep hand crack directly above (5.9) to a large ledge. Either traverse right into the corner of "Déja-Vu" or climb an easy break that leads slightly right to the base of a good grey slab. Move back left on big holds to a cam placement, then continue up the unprotectable slab (5.6) to belay off a large tree.

3. 45 m, 5.8+. Traverse under the flaring corner of "Déja-Vu" to a right-facing corner capped by a roof. Climb up the corner, then face climb up to the edge of the roof (fixed pitons) and continue into a prominent flake on the upper slab. Follow this to the top and the first treed ledge. Climb another short rock band to belay off trees.

Make a somewhat exposed traverse right (40 m) through steep trees to the top of the "Cyclops" bay.

Monster Mash 60 m, 5.9
D. Morgan & T. Friesen, 1982

According to Dave's rapidly waning memory, this climbs the wall just to the right of the arête that defines the left edge of the "Cyclops" bay. The details are lost but it "might have a crack to start and probably joins the arête higher up." Put some adventure back into your climbing and have a look, the rock looks great.

***Cyclops 70 m, 5.10b
A. Sole & G. Spohr, June 1978
Alternate first pitch: Adrian Burgess & E. Brooke

This is an original Ghost River classic that remains near the top of the heap for quality and character. Two different variations are available for the first pitch. Both are recommended and converge on the same belay. The climb finishes up a crack in the centre of a beautiful slab. The alternate first pitch was originally done as a mistake while looking for the route "Duveinafees." In a fit of poor memory, Nigel Hellewell was convinced that it climbed this crack, joined "Cyclops" at the belay, and finished out right. Thus, the original Chris Perry guide showed it as such. When Burgess and Brooke came to repeat "Duveinafees," a 5.7 route, and found hard 5.9 climbing, they realized something was amiss.

1. 40 m, 5.10a. The original route climbs the obvious crack on the left side of the bay. It has several overhanging sections that lead to a two-pin belay on a small stance below the upper slab on the right side.

1. alt. 40 m, 5.9. A slightly easier variation that climbs the corner crack right of the original route. It traverses left under a blocky, yellow overhang after about 15 m.

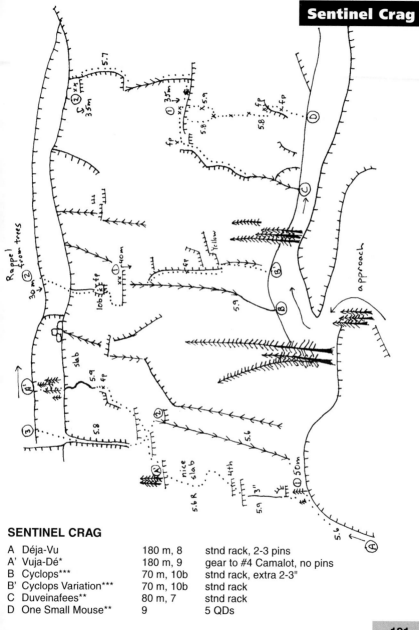

SENTINEL CRAG

A	Déja-Vu	180 m, 8	stnd rack, 2-3 pins
A'	Vuja-Dé*	180 m, 9	gear to #4 Camalot, no pins
B	Cyclops***	70 m, 10b	stnd rack, extra 2-3"
B'	Cyclops Variation***	70 m, 10b	stnd rack
C	Duveinafees**	80 m, 7	stnd rack
D	One Small Mouse**	9	5 QDs

Cyclops

Albi Sole on the first ascent of "Cyclops." Photo: Greg Spohr.

Sentinel Triangle

2. 30 m, 5.10b. Traverse left from the belay and then up to the horizontal edge. Traverse out to the edge to the obvious square ledge in the middle of the slab. Make a difficult mantle (piton, crux) and continue up the crack (awkward at first) to the top and a suitable belay tree some ways back from the lip. It is possible to bridge up the groove directly above the belay and then move left to the crux mantle.

**Duveinafees 80 m, 5.7
A. Sole & N. Hellewell, June 1978

For years, this climb suffered from confusion over its location (see "Cyclops" story above). Recent unearthing (literally) has rediscovered this very fine two-pitch crack climb. It begins in the major corner system just around right from" Cyclops."

1. 40 m, 5.7. Climb the corner (loose at first) to a fine layback crack that leads to a large overhang. Traverse right under the overhang to a mossy ledge. Scramble up to a higher ledge (piton) and traverse easily right for 5 m to a two-bolt belay.

2. 40 m, 5.7. Traverse right past a tree to a corner. Follow the nice corner to a large overhang and traverse right under the overhang into a splitter layback crack (recently unearthed). Follow this to a two-bolt belay on a ledge to the left.

**One Small Mouse 35 m, 5.9
B. Spear & J. Josephson, July 1996

This is a friction climb up the wall of excellent black rock to the left of "Duveinafees." Begin just left of a small cave 20 m right of the "Duveinafees" start. Climb up large jugs past a piton to a second piton (needs replacing with a bolt). Traverse left around an exposed arête to a stance and a bolt. Climb up past three more bolts with the crux mantle coming at the last bolt. Finish up an easy groove to the first bolt belay of "Duveinafees." From the third bolt it is possible to climb an unprotectable groove (5.8) to the left, bypassing the final bolt.

The Sentinel Triangle

Considering the vast amount of memory loss that has surrounded the routes of this crag, the authors couldn't help but ponder the existence of some ephemeral, magnetic field or substance that leads to chronic forgetfulness. It appears to be just like the "Bermuda Triangle," only different. Beware! As well as the "Duveinafees" story and the routes "Stretcher Case" and "Monster Mash" mentioned above, there are the following vague reports.

From Dave Morgan: Right of "Cyclops" and "Duveinafees" with Albi Sole, probably '82 or '83 called "Frosties."

From Peter Charkiw: A difficult roof above a large boulder that has 'God is Love' scrawled on it (the inscription is now difficult to read).

From Bill Stark: A couple of lines where the cliff meets the river; but no recollection of what, where or when they were climbed.

NORTH GHOST VALLEY

The north face of Sentinel Cliff (see page 182), Silver-Tongued Devil, Bastion Wall, Alberta Jam and Sunset Boulevard all lie at or beyond where the Ghost River makes a 90 degree turn to the west. Being farthest away from the Big Hill, it is understandably the least visited area.

Virtually all of the few routes in the area are recommended, which is understandable as the few forays into the region tend to pluck the best lines closest to the car. "Thor," "Alberta Jam" and "Sunset Boulevard" in particular might be three of the top five routes in the Ghost. Endless untouched cliffs extend west up the Ghost River, to the north along Johnson Creek and into the Waiparous region, as well as up most every side drainage and canyon.

Parking Access
From the canal bridge, continue north through some trees for 0.9 km to where a smaller road comes in from behind on the right. The east-facing Sentinel Cliff is directly above you at this point. To reach the crags continue for 500 m or so to where the river turns west and the road merges onto the rocky flood plain. Park here unless you are feeling particularly macho. Silver-Tongued Devil Crag is directly above you on the right.

SUNSET BOULEVARD

Sunset Boulevard crag lies on the south side of the river just over two km west of the North Ghost parking access at the 90 degree bend in the river. It is a large north-facing cliff consisting of a lower tier 40-80 m high and almost a kilometre long. This alone would be impressive if it weren't for the fact that the upper tier is just as long and closer to 200 metres high!

There are only three established routes on the lower tier and the upper cliff is unclimbed. "Sunset Boulevard" lies on the far left side of the cliff and its elegant arching dihedral (right-facing) cannot be missed. The other two routes are found right of the centre of the crag and both are mixed ice climbs called "Burning in Water, Drowning in Flame" and "The Sliver."

Dave Morgan was the first person to find and start on the unmistakable line of "Sunset Boulevard". He rappelled and cleaned the upper pitch and placed one bolt. However, he refused to top rope the pitch and set about establishing the climb from the ground up. Shortly after this, Andy Genereux spied the line and established the first pitch left of where Dave was working. On rappel he discovered Morgan's bolts. The two then embarked on a joint effort in which they were to take turns at establishing the upper pitch. Morgan refused to allow either one of them to do any "hanging or dogging."

The first day saw several attempts fail at the first crux. On the second day Andy finally overcame the technical difficulty of the lower crux and arrived at the second crux only to find he didn't have a carabiner to fit the homemade hanger Dave had previously fixed. This resulted in Andy launching into a 10 metre upside down fall and he relinquished the lead. Dave made it through the first crux but was unable to solve the second one. Andy had another turn, this time armed with the proper quick draw. To date there is no known second ascent of what became an instant classic.

Approach

Park at the bend in the river below Silver-Tongued Devil Crag. If you have a good 4WD with clearance you can often make it closer to the crag or even park at its base. Be forewarned that spring floods have been changing the road on a regular basis and the river crossings can be rather deep.

There is a river crossing right after the parking area that can usually be avoided on the left (south) bank. Continue upstream on an old road for about 30 minutes until almost at the end of a long straight section on the south side of the river. "Alberta Jam" is located across the river on a spectacular, vertically-tilted bedding plane. Photo page 199. "Sunset Boulevard" lies on the bottom tier of a layered north-facing cliff about 10 minutes upstream from "Alberta Jam." A short uphill hike deposits you below the route.

Descent

Walk off to the left or rappel with double ropes.

Dave Morgan attempting the incredible second pitch of "Sunset Boulevard."
Photo: Andy Genereux.

Sunset Boulevard

Sunset Boulevard

***Sunset Boulevard 70 m, 5.11c/d
A. Genereux & D. Morgan, 1987

The original Dave Morgan start is not currently used but it might be a better option as it would avoid the loose first half of pitch one.

1. 25 m, 5.10d. Climb a loose corner for 7 m and exit onto the face to a bolt. Good face climbing with the crux at the last bolt leads to the belay below the right-facing arch.
2. 45 m, 5.11c/d. At this point it is pretty obvious what to do next. Climb the superb dihedral with sustained cracks and stemming. Pull through a roof at the top and follow a short hand crack to a bolt belay.

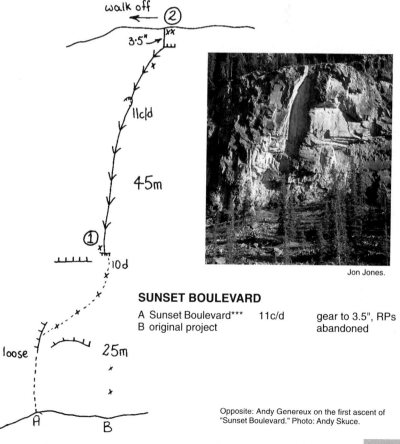

Jon Jones.

SUNSET BOULEVARD

A Sunset Boulevard***   11c/d   gear to 3.5", RPs
B original project   abandoned

Opposite: Andy Genereux on the first ascent of "Sunset Boulevard." Photo: Andy Skuce.

Alberta Jam

ALBERTA JAM

Like "Sunset Boulevard," if this route were in Yosemite, it would be frequently splashed across the glossies and be a world classic. But as it is, "Alberta Jam" sits in a Rockies backwater and has seen perhaps only four redpoint ascents. The biggest problem with this route is the lack of other climbs nearby and as the 11b/c crux is near the ground, you'll have little warm-up. There are numerous areas of good rock in the area but some of them look problematic to access. The wall just left of "Alberta Jam" looks inviting and deserves a few new routes.

Approach

Park at the bend in the river below Silver-Tongued Devil Crag. If you have a good 4WD with clearance you can often make it closer to the crag or even park at its base. Be forewarned that spring floods have been changing the road on a regular basis and the river crossings can be rather deep.

"Alberta Jam" is about 1.5 km west of the North Ghost parking area. There is a river crossing right after the parking area that can sometimes be avoided on the left (south) bank. Continue upstream on an old road for about 30 minutes until almost at the end of a long straight section on the south side of the river. "Alberta Jam" is located across the river on a spectacular, vertically-tilted bedding plane. The plane itself forms the right wall of a corner and faces southwest. It sits atop a scree slope and some broken ledges. See photo on right.

After crossing the stream it is another 30 minute uphill scree bash to reach a good ledge below the route. Avoid the climb in hot weather for the yellow rock in the corner acts as a brutal sun trap. But on the other hand, the climb can get unseasonably pleasant on a cold day if the sun is out.

The first ascent of "Alberta Jam" by Dave Morgan.
Photo: Greg Spohr, courtesy of The Sherwood House.

Alberta Jam

Recky Route 50 m, 5.8
G. Spohr & C. Yonge, 1982

Despite its obvious line, this is not a good route. It was done in one-and-a-half pitches and was climbed in order to explore the top of the bedding plane. Yonge recently recalled the climb, "It's not a great route and I recall the second pitch going leftish rather than right. I think the second pitch was only about 5.7 and grungy," strong comments from an expatriate Brit who tends to thrive on grungy climbs.

Part way up the corner there is an interesting traverse crack that curves right above and parallel to "Alberta Jam." It's doubtful that it has been climbed and it might make for a dramatic (and perhaps finer) finish to "Recky Route."

***Alberta Jam 50 m, 5.11b/c
D. Morgan, 1982

"Alberta Jam" was first discovered by Greg Spohr. Recognizing a classic when he saw one, Greg made somewhat of an effort to climb it. He soon realized he needed bigger guns and brought in Dave Morgan and Chas Yonge. The route was originally aided in order to clean out loose rock in the upper crack. All further efforts at free climbing were done on lead. It was Morgan who managed the first redpoint after a number of efforts. Sean Dougherty made the second ascent and Chas Yonge the third (at the age of 40). Andy Genereux is the only other person known to have redpointed the route, which has yet to see an on-sight ascent.

The technical crux of the route is found within the first 10 metres. (There have been numerous episodes of "down-aiding" to retreat.) One of the challenges is picking the right gear for the leaning, off-set crack. It has ample places for good protection but exactly which piece goes where is not obvious. Milk a deserved rest in the pod where the crack turns upwards. Launch skyward in the more straightforward jam crack until the wall tilts to slightly overhanging some distance from the top.

Rappel the route. There is a two-bolt anchor but no chains. Bring a new sling to replace the rat-licked leftovers on this rarely travelled test piece.

Alberta Jam

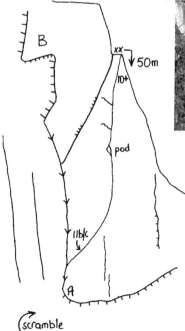

ALBERTA JAM

A Alberta Jam***   11b/c   lots of gear to 3.5"
B Recky Route   50 m, 8   gear to 4"

Alberta Jam

Thunder Thigh Crack 125 m, 5.9
K. Nagy, F. Campbell & J. A. Owen, Sept. 1986

This route faces due south and is found out on the prowlike buttress before the cliff disintegrates into the Valley of the Birds. Although considerably larger than the Alberta Jam formation, the west-facing, inverted bedding plane to the left of "Thunder Thigh Crack" remains unexplored.

Approach
The top of the route can be easily identified by a 30 m-long, left-facing dihedral. Climb a short scree slope immediately above the creek past a massive boulder to the base of the route. The first three pitches have the occasional 5.6 move. The team performed a lot of cleaning but still expect to find occasional loose sections. Several #11 Hexes or tube chocks are useful for off-width.

1. 35 m, 5.6. Start immediately above the big boulder. Climb the steep blocky wall trending slightly left to a good ledge with a boulder and small shrub.
2. 30 m, 5.6. Climb diagonally up and right for 6 m past a short wall to an easy groove that is followed for 12 m to an easy gully. Go up the gully trending left to a big ledge below a steep wall.
3. 30 m, 5.6. Pass the steep wall by going right up a groove to a small ledge. Traverse left along the ledge and climb the blocky face to another good ledge below the obvious corner crack.
4. 30 m, 5.9. Climb the crack that goes from hand to fist to off-width and gets progressively steeper and harder. Near the top, step around left to a loose ledge and go across easy slabs for 7 m to an old tree.

Descent
Walk over a treed ridge heading east toward the Valley of the Birds and go diagonally down toward the main valley staying in the trees all the way.

SILVER-TONGUED DEVIL CRAG

This attractive cliff rises directly above the Ghost River where it makes a 90 degree turn to the west. It is named after the first route on the cliff, which is actually a waterfall ice climb. The Silver-Tongued Devil (STD) comes from a distinct cave halfway up the cliff on the left end. All of the routes reported here are in the vicinity of this cave. As this wall faces due south and is relatively low, it has one of the longest seasons of any cliff in the area. People have regularly climbed here into October.

Right of STD the cliff takes a slight turn to the east and becomes very grey and rippled. It is a fine-looking cliff with numerous corners in the upper half. Kelly Tobey and Frank Campbell have both done routes on this section but neither of them remember much about them. Frank did one short route that ends in a cave about 30 m right of STD and he and Orvil Miskiw did a two-pitch route that climbs 5.9 face with a 5.8 groove above. Kelly remembers nothing of the route(s) he did. Unfortunately, this is the only information that remains.

Chas Yonge and partner followed a route just to the left of the Silver-Tongued Devil smear in order to reach the cave and check on spelunking opportunities. Rappelling off "Hoods in the Woods" you might see some fixed pitons (see topo on page 206) from this route but it is not recommended. By the way, despite having a nearly flat floor, the cave is nothing more than a frost pocket and extends only a few metres into the cliff. There is a fixed station on the left wall of the cave that is used to rappel the waterfall climb.

Approach

Park in the cobblestone flats where the river turns west. This is referred to as the North Ghost Parking Access, see page 194 for details. It may be possible to drive across the river and follow an old road in the trees. Park somewhere directly below the crag. Flagging tape on the north side of the road indicates a short trail that leads through the trees to the hillside below the crag. Frank Campbell generously removed much of the deadfall that blocked the way. Head more or less straight up the hillside bypassing some small rocky steps. Thirty-40 minutes of uphill slogging puts you at a nice ledge below the Silver-Tongued Devil.

Descent

Descend "Rabid Crack" by walking to the left and scrambling down through the trees and back to the base.

"Hoods in the Woods" and "Devil's Eye" are descended via two 50 m rappels. The top anchor is a single bolt backed up by a good natural thread. It is required to carry replacement rappel sling because the rats will undoubtedly take care of what is left.

Silver-Tongued Devil Crag

**Rabid Crack 100 m, 5.8
First ascent unknown.

This could be one of the Kelly Tobey routes that he no longer remembers. The name was applied later by Joe Josephson after his finger was bitten by a bat that had taken residence in the crack on the second pitch. A fine route with good crack climbing. Start about 10 m left of the Silver-Tongued Devil.

1. 55 m, 5.7. Climb up an easy slab to a large ledge below a nice corner. If you have short ropes it may be wise to belay here. Climb the corner up and left to a fixed piton in the crack just before the corner turns more sharply to the left. Traverse right across a steep grey wall and climb up a short wall to a small ledge with a large block. Follow the top edge of a huge flake left and up to a small ledge with a two-bolt belay.

2. 45 m, 5.8. Move left from the belay going up a short slab until you can make a difficult step right on to a small ledge below the upper corner and about 5 m above the belay. Climb up the corner and around the "bat bulge" (5.8) and continue up the corner to a small roof. Either climb the roof directly (5.8) or traverse onto an unprotectable slab of good rock to the left (5.6). Either route takes you to a large ledge with some small trees and a possible belay. If you don't mind some rope drag, traverse left for 10 m or so to a tree below a loose corner. Climb the corner to the top.

**Hoods in the Woods 90 m, 5.10b
F. Campbell & L. Terras, June 1988

This takes the intimidating yellow wall between "Rabid Crack" and the Silver-Tongued Devil. The second pitch traverses right into the obvious corner crack directly above the STD cave. The first pitch is 5.9 and rates as one of the finer pitches of that grade. The second, crux pitch is also good despite being awkward in the upper corner.

1. 50 m, 5.9. A few metres right of the Silver-Tongued Devil climb up easy broken ground to a slab with a horizontal break. Continue up the slab to an old bolt. Either climb straight up from the bolt to the edge of a left-facing corner or alternatively, move left immediately from the bolt and then go straight up (5.8, small wires or RPs) to the corner, which is followed (fixed pitons) to a small ledge at the top. Climb the steep yellow wall above (5.9) past a bolt and into a right-facing corner. Struggle up the corner until easier ledges lead right to a fixed cable anchor.

2. 40 m, 5.10b. Step right from the belay and then up a large yellow scoop to a bolt. Continue up and right (10a) past two more bolts that lead onto grey rock and a large corner. Climb the increasingly and surprisingly difficult corner (10b, large cams helpful) for 25 m to a large ledge on the right. Belay off a bolt and a good natural thread to the right.

Silver-Tongued Devil Crag

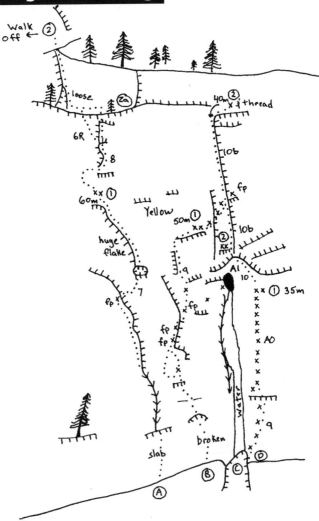

SILVER-TONGUED DEVIL CRAG

A Rabid Crack**   8   stnd rack
B Hoods in the Woods**   10b   stnd rack, one large piece
C Silver-Tongued Devil   water ice grade 5
D Devil's Eye*   10b, A1   stnd rack, extra biners

Silver-Tongued Devil Crag

*Devil's Eye 90 m, 5.10b, A1
F. Campbell & R. Banard, June 1991

Directly above the STD cave there is a large roof with a crack splitting it. Wishing to check it out, Frank Campbell began a bolt ladder up the water streak right of the STD waterfall. Frank made many efforts to establish the bolt ladder, which was drilled by hand and often times solo when he couldn't find partners for other projects. More natural aid pulled the roof above the cave and led into the upper corner taken by "Hoods in the Woods." The roof has a bunch of fixed gear and would likely go free. The position on the roof over the cave is unbeatable. Although not as steep, the bolt ladder would be a considerably harder challenge to free climb (5.13?). It does, however, have immaculate, compact rock with more protection than you could ever hope for. Good luck! Begin immediately right of Silver-Tongued Devil.

1. 35 m, 5.9 A0. Excellent climbing (5.9) up a steep slab leads past four bolts to a silver streak just right of the water smear. Climb the bolt ladder for 20 m to a bolt belay below a large overhang and about level with the cave.
2. 10 m, 5.10 A1. Climb a left-leaning crack in the overhangs above. Free and aid moves along the crack lead to the big roof directly over the cave. Aid the roof and continue free to a small ledge on the left with a two-bolt belay.
2. 45 m, 5.10b. Climb the corner (10b) to a small ledge where "Hoods in the Woods" traverses in from the left. Continue up the corner (10b) to the belay ledge on the right.

Unclimbed Right Side

BASTION WALL

This aptly named cliff begins just north of Silver-Tongued Devil Crag and extends a considerable distance (almost 5 km!) to the north around the base of Devil's Head Mountain (see map page 184). The rock is among the best in the area but there are few natural lines and only seven routes have been climbed to date. Of these, only "Thor" has seen sufficient activity to warrant a star rating. Not enough is known about the others although some of them look very good. All are located on the south end within the first kilometre. Ian Bolt and Dan Guthrie did two routes somewhere left of "Thor," but details were lost, however, when the pair perished in an avalanche in Alaska. Farther north near the waterfall routes "Sorcerer" and "Hydrophobia," the cliff contains massive towers and sweeping, blank faces. A French climber who once saw the cliffs refused to believe there were no rock climbs on these walls. He declared that in France there would be over a thousand routes. Well, this ain't France and there they sit, *sain et sauf* (untouched).

Approach
Park in the cobblestone flats where the Ghost River turns west. This is referred to as the North Ghost Parking Access, see page 194 and map page 144 for details. It may be possible to drive across the river and park near a meadow that marks the start of the approach trail. The trail (actually an old road) begins steeply as it heads north between Bastion Wall to the left and Black Rock Mountain to the right.

Climbs near the west end can be reached by leaving the road just before the top of the final steep section and heading up a ridge that is partially open at first and then more treed higher up. This comes out close to "Thor."

The traditional approach, however, is to continue up the road to the gully below "Satan," which can then be followed to the base of the cliff with a minimum of bushwhacking.

Descent
Since the cliff extends a long way to the north, the only feasible descent is at the west end. A bench at the top of the cliff can be followed past "Thor" and "Lucky for Some" to a good tree at the edge. See photo on page 210. Two 45 m ropes just reach the base of the cliff. Alternatively, traverse at a higher level farther west and scramble down the break in the cliff bands between Bastion Wall and Silver-Tongued Devil Crag.

At the west end of the wall, to the left of "Thor," there are a number of short crack and corner lines. The farthest right of these, at the beginning of the main wall, is "Lucky for Some," a prominent, right-facing crack and chimney system. Immediately left of this is a groove that begins at a ledge part way up the cliff and is climbed by "Lugey's Copter." To the left again, also starting from the ledge, is the steep, flaring corner/crack of "Larry, Curly and Mo."

Bastion Wall

Lugey's Copter 70 m, 5.8
A. Pickel & T. Back, July 1982

Begin to the left of the upper groove noted above, below a short, left-facing chimney. Pitch 2 is sustained and on good rock.
1. 25 m, 5.6. Climb the chimney to a large ledge. Move right along the ledge for about 6 m and then step down to belay below the groove.
2. 45 m, 5.8. Climb the steep groove above for about 12 m and then move left and continue up the face. After about 6 m, move back right into the groove and follow it to the top of the cliff.

Larry, Curly and Mo 65 m, 5.9
S. Dougherty, C. Quinn & D. Cheesmond, 1985

Begin as for "Lugey's Copter" at the short, left-facing chimney.
1. 25 m, 5.6. Go up the chimney and then move up and left to belay below the flaring corner/crack.
2. 40 m, 5.9. Climb the corner to ledges at the top.

Lucky for Some 100 m, 5.6
A. Sole & N. Hellewell, 1978

Follow the crack and chimney system described above for three pitches of 5.6 climbing. The name is derived from an incident on the first ascent when Nigel Hellewell fell off while climbing solo. Fortunately, he landed on Albi Sole who was directly below and who managed to hold both of them!

Bastion Wall Descent

A. Thor
O Rappel Descent

Bastion Wall

***Thor 145 m, 5.10a
N. Hellewell & J. Upton, July 1977

"Thor" follows the obvious shallow corner near the south end of the main cliff. It is one of the best climbs in the area and a number of repeat ascents have confirmed its quality. The climbing is sustained and on excellent rock but good protection is sometimes difficult to arrange, notably on the first pitch and the beginning of the second. Take a good selection of gear (up to #3.5 Friend).

1. 45 m, 5.10a. Follow the groove with continuous interest and awkward protection to a small stance and bolt belay.

2. 30 m, 5.10a. Make a few moves left and up to gain a short ramp that leads back right. The ramp ends in a shallow, steepening scoop, above which difficult bridging past old, dubious pitons leads to a steep chimney. Continue up to a small ledge about 5 m below a blank-looking bulge.

3. 50 m, 5.9. Climb the groove to a bolt on the right and continue up over the bulge. Hard, sustained climbing leads to a ledge near the top of the cliff.

4. 20 m. Continue to the top and belay at a tree higher up.

Satan 200 m, 5.10b
N. Hellewell & F. O'Sullivan, July 1977

When walking north along the road, the first really prominent line is a huge corner above a shallow gully in the hillside. "Satan" goes up the corner and has some interesting climbing in its lower section particularly on the pitch leading to the upper corner.

Climb the right side of the bowl beneath the corner moving left near the top to a bolt belay beneath overhangs (5.8). Traverse right to a crack through the overhangs and climb this (5.9) and the groove above to a ledge beneath an overhanging chimney. Climb the overhanging chimney and the steep groove above (5.10b). Several pitches of less difficult climbing (up to 5.8) lead to the top.

Leprechaun 210 m, 5.9, A0
J. Firth & T. Jones, July 1977

"Leprechaun" climbs a discontinuous corner system in the upper part of the buttress to the right of "Satan" and left of a large bay. The climb can be seen on the approach at the break in the trees by a distinctive stump some 6 m high and 30 m from the highest elevation of the road. On the grey wall directly ahead are three yellow patches; "Leprechaun" ascends a lower corner system below the central yellow patch and traverses across right to gain the second of two upper corners, which is then followed to the top. It has some excellent climbing especially on the last two pitches.

1-3. Three pitches of 5.6-5.7 climbing lead to a ledge on the left near the base of the lower corner.

4. 5.9. Climb the corner past the first roof. Move left to avoid a steep section and traverse back into the corner on the ramp above. Belay beneath a second open book.

Bastion Wall

5. 50 m, 5.7. Climb the corner and the wall above.
6. 50 m, 5.9, A0. Climb progressively steepening rock up and right to the base of a groove capped by an overhang. Move right across a slabby wall and up to a prominent corner. Climb this to a nut (in place) and tension right to a crack below a second corner. Follow this, using three pitons for aid near the top to a good ledge. The pitch will likely go free at about 5.10c.
7. 5.7. Climb up the overhanging crack to the top.

Loki 210 m, 5.6
N. Hellewell & M. Talbot, May 1980

Located on the right wall of the bay to the north of "Leprechaun" is a chimney line with a left-slanting overhang at about one-third height. The climb follows the obvious line all the way except for an optional detour onto slabs on the left at about half height.

Left: Nigel Hellewell on the first attempt of "Satan." Photo: Chris Perry.

Opposite: Photo from the cover of the original 1980 "Ghost River Rock" guide. Bruce Keller attempting a new route on Bastion Wall. Over 15 years later, the route remains unclimbed. Photo: Chris Perry.

Bastion Wall

Waiparous Creek

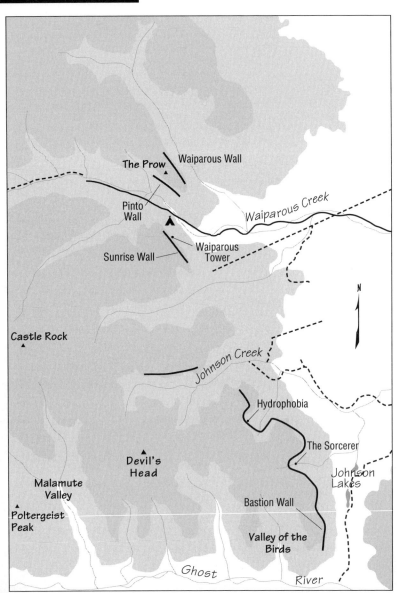

WAIPAROUS CREEK

The Waiparous Creek valley is the next major drainage north of the Ghost River. It has impressive cliff bands, similar to those in the Ghost, but they are less extensive and there are essentially only three major cliffs in the central climbing area. The rock is exceptional by local standards and there are a number of interesting features and impressive walls. However, the approach is difficult, being either a long walk or a true 4WD experience. Accessing Waiparous Creek makes the Ghost River approach seem easy.

All climbing routes to date have been established by Frank Campbell and a small group of friends who have had the area to themselves. Only the obvious lines have been climbed and there are large sections of untouched rock, most notably the entire, 300-400 m high east face of The Prow known as "Waiporous Wall." The routes done to date feature mainly crack climbing, often at a good standard and on excellent rock. Pitons are worth taking on most of the climbs.

Approach

Continue north on Forestry Trunk Road 940 past the Ghost River turnoff at the Bar Cee Ranch and into the forest reserve. 13.2 km north of the forest boundary, turn left (west) onto Waiparous Valley Road. Drive past Camp Mockingbird to a junction at 2.8 km. Turn left on to a rougher road (signed Margaret Lake trail), which is passable for another 4 km through Hidden Creek and past Camp Howard and Camp Chamisall. At the foot of a deeply-trenched hill, turn left into a parking area by the creek. At this point it is necessary to either start walking/biking or lock the hubs on the trusty 4WD. After the hill the road descends back down to Waiparous Creek and then twines around a driveable cutline for a further 6.8 km to the Margaret Lake junction (follow the yellow OHV and snowmobile signs in this section). Cross over to the south bank of Waiparous Creek and continue on the "road" through several river crossings for about a further 4 km (excellent views of The Prow). A steep climb over a boulder-studded hill at a bend in the river leads to a final crossing and a good camping area between Pinto Wall and Sunrise Wall.

Sunrise Wall

A. Concord
B. Waiparous Tower & The Finger

SUNRISE WALL

Sunrise Wall is a long, east-facing cliff that extends south from the upper Waiparous Valley. A large, block-like tower is a prominent feature near the right-hand end.

Gutbuster 95 m, 5.9
F. Campbell and J. A. Owen, Oct. 1987

Gutbuster climbs an obvious, right-facing corner system at the extreme south end of the wall. It begins at a large treed ledge, about one pitch up the face, which can be reached by scrambling up from the left.

1. 40 m, 5.9. Climb the lower corner to a two-bolt belay on the right.
2. 45 m, 5.9. Move up and left into the continuation corner and climb this to ledges on the left at the top.

***Concord 190 m, 5.10d
F. Campbell and R. Banard, Aug. 1996

This excellent climb goes up a corner system roughly in the centre of the wall and about 250 m south of the tower. In the lower section it climbs a prominent, clean-cut open book that faces right and begins about 10 m up the wall.

Take plenty of crack gear, up to #4 Friend.

1. 35 m, 5.9. Climb up to the base of the open book and continue up an excellent finger crack in the left wall to a ledge just left of a wide crack (two-bolt belay).
2. 45 m, 5.9. Climb the upper portion of the open book to a fixed station at a small ledge on the left wall.
3. 15 m, 5.10a. Traverse back into the corner and climb a crack to a large roof. Go out right around this and up to easier ground. Belay at a ledge on the left where the open book ends (piton).
4. 45 m, 5.10d. Follow a crack up through a bulge past two bolts to an overhang. Climb a notch in the overhang and go up to a second overhang (bolts). Traverse right for 2 m and climb directly up to a two-bolt belay where the angle eases.
5. 50 m, 5.10a. Climb up to a rib on the left and go up this to a ledge (bolts). Move up to the top of a small pinnacle and then go up just right of an overhang to a steep wall. Follow a crack system up the wall to a two-bolt belay at the top.

Descent: Rappel the route using the fixed stations at the top of pitches 5, 4, 2 and 1.

Sunrise Wall

Waiparous Tower - South Side 130 m, 5.8
F. Campbell and J. A. Owen, Oct. 1987

This aesthetic, clean-cut formation is a prominent feature near the north end of the wall. Only the inside face on the south side has been climbed although other possibilities exist, most notably on the north edge. Photos on page 8 and opposite page.

The climb starts in the gully on the south side of the tower at a crack on the right wall.

1. 50 m, 5.8. Climb the crack to a ledge, move left and climb a chimney to easier ground. Move up to a ledge below a continuation corner system.
2. 50 m, 5.8. Climb the corner/crack moving slightly right toward a pinnacle on the edge. Continue up left following a corner to a ledge level with a traverse line leading right on to the front face of the tower.
3. 5 m, 5.7. Make a steep, exposed traverse right to a ledge and piton belay on the front face.
4. 25 m, 5.7. Climb the steep face above on good holds but minimal protection past a piton to a ledge system that leads right and up to the top.

Descent: Rappel from a large block on the summit (long sling required) into the notch between the tower and the main wall. A 50 m rappel reaches a single bolt station about 10 m above the notch. Rappel again into the notch and then scramble down the gully on the north side.

***The Finger - Right Side 145 m, 5.10b**
F. Campbell, S. McDonald and S. Brucke, July 1988

"The Finger" is an obvious feature a short distance right of the tower. It begins at about two-thirds height, rises almost to the top of the cliff, and has impressive cracks on both its north and south sides. The quality of the rock hereabouts is exceptional and the last two pitches of the climb give some of the best, hard crack climbing in the guidebook area.

Start directly below The Finger at a right-facing corner system that curves over to the left.

1. 50 m, 5.7. Follow the corner system up and left to a corner crack that leads up to a belay at a block below an overhang.
2. 25 m, 5.8. Climb the overhang to gain an alcove above (5.8) and then make an exposed, horizontal traverse right to a short groove below the right-hand side of The Finger.
3. 20 m, 5.10a. Move up and then across right with difficulty to reach a break through the bulging wall above. Go up this and then over left to the base of the crack on the right side of The Finger.
4. 25 m, 5.9. Excellent crack climbing in the corner past several overhangs leads to a fixed rappel station at a small ledge on the right wall.
5. 25 m, 5.10b. Continue up the crack on superb rock to the top of the pinnacle (two-bolt belay).

Descent: Rappel to the station at the top of pitch 4 and then make two long rappels past a second station on the wall below the end of the long traverse—see photo.

PINTO WALL

This colourful wall faces almost due south and parallels the creekbed. Only three climbs have been established to date, all near the upper, right-hand end. They follow prominent right-facing corner systems that begin just down and left of the highest point of a long scree slope. "Golden Cherub" is the classic of the crag and this follows a system of chimneys and corners directly to the top of the cliff.

Approach: From the campsite area, cross the river and climb easy, open slopes directly to the base of the routes.

Descent: Walk north and west to avoid cliff bands and then drop down into the drainage at the west end of the crag.

A. Golden Cherub Area

**Fun Yet? 230 m, 5.7
M. Toft, F. Campbell and J. A. Owen, June 1988

"Fun Yet?" and "Compressor Fumes" are both reached by scrambling up and left across relatively easy ground from just below the high point of the scree slope. They begin at a long, horizontal ledge just over one third of the way up the cliff. "Fun Yet?" climbs an obvious, right-facing corner system that diagonals up left and it is the farthest west of the three climbs.

1. 5.6. From the ledge, move left and climb a corner. Go left again and then up into the base of the main corner (two-bolt belay).
2-3. 5.7. Climb the corner/crack for two pitches to a belay near the top.
4. Climb easily to the top.

Pinto Wall

*Compressor Fumes 225 m, 5.9
F. Campbell, S. McDonald and S. Brucke, July 1988

This interesting route follows a corner system on the wall to the right of "Fun Yet?" It gives several pitches of good, sustained crack climbing.

Begin below and right of the upper corner system, at the long ledge noted above in the description for "Fun Yet?"

1. 30 m, 5.7. Climb a corner, move right and then go diagonally up left to the main corner system.
2. 35 m, 5.8. Follow the corner up to a ledge.
3. 45 m, 5.9. Continue up the corner system to where it eases near the top of the cliff.
4. 15 m. Exit up a short chimney.

Pinto Wall – Golden Cherub Area

A. Fun Yet?
B. Compressor Fumes
C. Golden Cherub

Pinto Wall

***Golden Cherub 190 m, 5.9+
F. Campbell and D. Dancer, Sept. 1987

Start to the right of the previous two routes below a right-facing groove that curves over left to the base of the lower chimney. Take a good selection of large gear.
1. 25 m, 5.7. Climb the groove to a piton belay at the base of the chimney.
2. 40 m, 5.8. Climb the chimney past a fixed piton inside to a ledge (large gear required).
3. 45 m, 5.9+. Go diagonally up and right on easy ground to a ledge. Move right and climb a right-facing corner/crack to a belay below a wide chimney.
4. 45 m, 5.9+. Climb the chimney and move out right at the top to a grassy ledge and piton at the base of a right-facing corner. Climb the corner past a piton until an overhang blocks the way. An exposed traverse leads left to loose blocks in a major crack system. Climb the crack with difficulty to a small ledge.
5. 35 m, 5.8. Continue up the gully to the top.

THE PROW

"The Prow" is the name given to a huge buttress of rock situated between Waiparous Creek and its north fork. It marks the southern end of a long line of east-facing cliffs that extends northward for some distance and are marked on the area map as "Waiparous Wall." The first section of cliff, which is readily visible on the approach, presents one of the most inviting pieces of unclimbed rock in the guidebook area. There appears to be a number of possible lines on this 300-400 m face and the rock looks good. An inspirational photograph is included as an invitation to all would-be first ascensionists. Hurry up, Frank—get back on there and finish your route off!

THE ANTI-GHOST

As the name may imply, this venue is not really in the Ghost River. This east-facing cliff sits above the Ghost Valley as an extension to a south ridge on Black Rock Mountain. The cliff is visible only at a few locations along the access road, notably at a T-junction 4.6 km before the top of the Big Hill. It is totally non-visible from the Ghost itself. When this cliff was first explored, there were big hopes for a new venue without the rigourous approach endemic to the rest of the region. Those hopes were quickly lost with the long walk required to reach the crag and the scrappy nature of the rock itself. Only two small pockets have produced routes of any quality. Steep slopes directly below the climbs make it a bit of a thrutch to move around near the base. Don't drop your pack! These are worth considering if you discover the Ghost River too high to cross or when a cold wind is blowing in the lower valleys.

There are two sections of the cliff where climbs have been established and these are marked on the accompanying photograph. At the south end is the Motocross Crack area where two climbs have been done, one on each side of a prominent gully. The other section that has been developed is the Bluebell Crack area situated in a prominent bay just right of the centre of the crag.

Parking Access & Approach

About 100 m before the top of the Big Hill, a dirt road heads off north and, after about 300 m, enters a large meadow and campsite area. From here, the cliff can be readily seen in profile to the north. The road continues but deteriorates rapidly and it is best to proceed on foot or mountain bike for about a kilometre to a small hill where a horse trail branches off to the right toward the cliff. Follow this to a steep hill that has been gouged by motocross riders. Scrap up the hill and continue north along a treed bench below the cliff. A short uphill gouge will put you at the base of the cliff. The approach takes about an hour.

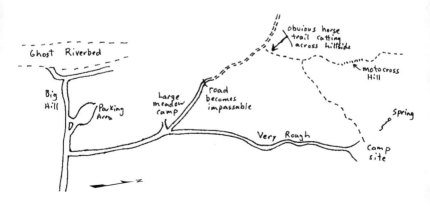

The Anti-Ghost

A. Motocross Crack area
B. Bluebell Crack area

224

Motocross Crack Area

*Chinook 20 m, 5.10d
F. Campbell, K. Doyle & Y. Leduc, May 1989

"Chinook" climbs the clean corner, capped by a roof, to the left of the prominent gully. Some gear is required for the lower corner.

1. 20 m, 5.10d. Climb the corner to the roof (5.9) and go out right to a bolt. Move over the overhang with difficulty (5.10d) past a piton and up into a short groove. Climb the groove and continue up and slightly left past more pitons (5.10a) to a good tree at the top.

Motocross Crack 20 m, 5.9
F. Campbell & M. Brolsma, 1988

This route climbs the obvious groove to the right of the gully and requires a small selection of gear.

Descent: Descend both routes by walking off the back of the cliff to the south.

Bluebell Crack Area

All the routes here are descended by rappel. One 50 m rope is adequate.

**Bluebell Crack 15 m, 5.10a
F. Campbell and M. Brolsma, 1987

Excellent, albeit short, crack. Either lower off the first single bolt or traverse left on a somewhat creaking flake to a small tree.

**Bluebell Extension 22 m, 5.11c
A. Genereux and S. Mascioli, 1995

A desperate face climbing finish to Bluebell Crack.

Bluebell Corner 25 m, 5.9
F. Campbell and T. Mooney, 1987

It is unsure where the first ascentionist belayed but it is now recommended to traverse left to the bolt belay of "Bluebell Extension." If the crack was clean of vegetation, it would be rather nice. At present, however, the corner is quite dirty.

Handiwork 20 m, 5.9
FRA: S. Mascioli & A. Genereux, 1995

Immediately right of "Bluebell Corner" there is an obvious hand crack. It is rather loose near the top but could become a good route if it was cleaned up.

Bluebell Crack Area

The Handle 20 m, 5.8
FRA: A. Genereux & S. Mascioli, 1995

A twin route to the right of the previous climb but a grade easier.

*City View 18 m, 5.11d
A. Genereux, 1995

A devious arête with hard face climbing on somewhat friable edges.

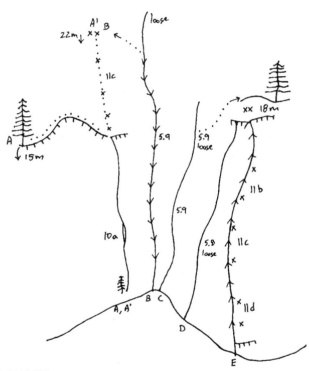

THE ANTI-GHOST

Bluebell Crack Area
A	Bluebell Crack**	10a	gear to 2.5"
A'	Bluebell Extension**	11c	gear to 2.5"
B	Bluebell Corner	9	gear to 3"
C	Handiwork	9	gear to 3.5"
D	The Handle	8	gear to 3.5"
E	City View*	11d	6 QDs

ALPINE ROCK

This is the beginning of what we hope is an ever-expanding chapter. Part of the wildness and scenery of the Ghost lies above the cliffs that grace the toes of the mountains. Over the years, numerous forays have been made into the upper reaches of the mountains and it is surprising how recently many of the peaks have received their first ascent. There is likely to be several (if not more) peaks or bumps on the ridges that remain totally unclimbed. As well, an almost endless supply of unexplored ridges and faces will undoubtedly burp up many more interesting routes of a general mountaineering bent. Here we have included the most technical of the completed climbs along with a variety of thigh-busting scrambles/climbs from the now out-of-print *Rocky Mountains of Canada South* by Glen Boles.

All of the climbs mentioned here lie north of the Minnewanka Valley (Palliser Range) and are on the Lake Minnewanka map sheet 82-O/6. To convert metre readings into feet (elevations on the map sheet are in feet), divide metres by 0.3048.

Orient Point, Saddle Peak and several unnamed points on the south side of the valley (northern end of the Fairholme Range) should present some interesting scrambles/climbs for those so inclined. See *Rocky Mountains of Canada South* and the Canmore map sheet 82-O/3 for more details.

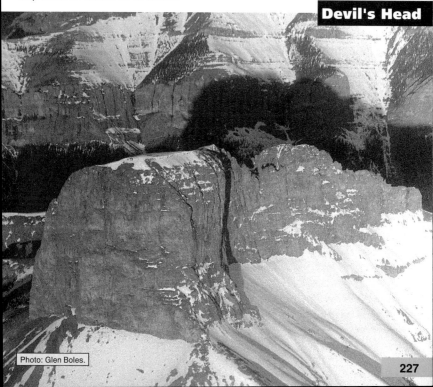

Devil's Head

Photo: Glen Boles.

Alpine Rock

Phantom Crag Summits

A long ridge line extends westward from above the main climbing areas to the summit of Mount Costigan. Two rocky summits sit on top of this ridge at its eastern end and offer some interest to rock climbers "with a mountaineering problem." The eastern summit is marked as "Phantom Crag" (GR 265836, elevation 2,275 m) and its imposing east side is shown on the photograph of South Phantom Crag (page 114). To the authors' knowledge the peak has not been climbed from this side. West Phantom Crag Summit is a sister formation that lies about a kilometre to the west (GR 254837, elevation 2,365 m) and is not visible from many of the normal viewpoints. The two summits look very much alike and can be confused. From the Minnewanka Valley, the east summit sits directly above the Bonanza drainage whereas the west summit lies above the Aquarius/Recital Hall drainage. Both summits can be easily reached via their west sides and only the west summit has been climbed by its east ridge. This climb is reported to be a worthwhile outing.

*East Ridge of West Phantom Crag Summit, 5.6
F. Campbell, P. Roxburgh & D. White, 1984

The climb begins at the col between the east and west summits. This can be reached from Wully Canyon by hiking up the drainage that serves as part of the descent from North Phantom Crag (see approach) and descent details on page 159). Alternatively, East Gully (page 159 and then the South Phantom Crag descent gully (page 148) can be used to access the upper slopes. The ridge itself gives two pitches of 5.6 climbing on good rock and leads directly to the west summit. Descent can be made down the easy west side of the peak and then north down a relatively open drainage that leads back to the Ghost River just west of Sentinel Cliff (GR 245864). A much shorter descent can be made down the approach drainage although this requires a rappel. From the summit, scramble down to the north and locate a piton at the north end of a small cliff band. A 20 m rappel and easy scrambling allow the drainage to be reached, which is then followed down to Wully Canyon.

A. Thunder God Buttress, Mount Costigan
B. East Phantom Crag Summit

Alpine Rock

Costigan's Boil (2,564 m, 8,410 ft.)

This aptly-named peak is on the ridge line that extends from the main summit of Mount Costigan east to Phantom Crag (GR 232834). It is a somewhat technical, blocky "boil" that sticks up above the surrounding scree slopes. The first (and perhaps only) ascent came in August 1960 by P. Duffy, J. K. Gray, Mr. and Mrs. Heinz Kahl. From *Rocky Mountains of Canada South*:

"From Devil's Gap pass Phantom Lake to the second canyon on the north side of the valley [Lacy Gibbet drainage]. Hike and climb up this canyon to its head bypassing two waterfalls [Lacy Gibbet?] to trees above canyon wall, one hour through forest. Follow steep meadows to ridge in one hour. This ridge runs east to Phantom Crag. Follow the ridge west staying on the north side and use the rope again near the top. Descend by the same route. (*CAJ Volume 44, page 55*)"

Mount Costigan (2,980 m, 9,775 ft.)

Mount Costigan lies at the top of the long ridge line that extends west from the Phantom Crag summits. The first recorded ascent came in June 1975 from the "Grizzly Group" of Don Forest, Gordon Scruggs and Glen Boles. Their description is from *Rocky Mountains of Canada South* page 432:

"From camp above canyon, below long south ridge, hiked up slopes west of south ridge to about 2,450 m, then traversed northwest over two ridges then climbed ledges and bands interspersed with scree to southwest ridge, ridge to summit. Found cairn and survey marker, 7 hours. Descend via southwest slopes and canyon, 2.5 hours. (*CAJ Volume 59, page 83*)."

Mount Costigan has a very impressive northeast buttress that can be seen from the top of the Big Hill or from the entrance to the Minnewanka Valley (see photo page 60). The buttress was first climbed by Frank Campbell and J. A. Owen and was named "Thunder God Buttress" to commemorate a rapid, unplanned, lightning-induced descent from the summit into the Minnewanka Valley. This resulted in a long hike back to their car which was in the North Ghost, giving a round trip of 25 km!

Thunder God Buttress is a prominent feature of the Minnewanka valley and the climb is included here despite its limited appeal to most Ghost River clientele. Perhaps a fun day out, which could be called the "Ghost River Integral," would be to climb the South Face of Phantom Tower, continue over the east and west Phantom Crag summits and Costigan's Boil, and then climb the Thunder God Buttress to the summit of Mount Costigan.

Thunder God Buttress 250 m, 5.9

F. Campbell & J. A. Owen, Aug. 1986

The original approach was via the northeast drainage of Mount Costigan. To access from this direction, continue up the Ghost River past the "Alberta Jam" and "Sunset Boulevard" crags to a major valley on the south side (GR 206866). Head south up the valley and then angle left to gain the col between Costigan's Boil and the northeast buttress just to the west of a large block (GR 217834). A more logical approach, how-

Alpine Rock

ever, is from the Minnewanka Valley as the easiest descent from the summit is in that direction. Costigan's Boil is a small summit immediately east of the col that can be climbed (fourth class) by its east ridge. Access to this ridge from the Minnewanka Valley can be made easily via the major canyon beyond the Aquarius/Recital Hall drainage. The canyon is located just beyond the second Ghost Lake (GR 235811) and is home to a number of ice climbs including the long and popular "Lacy Gibbet."

From the col climb a step (5.7) on good rock to the base of the main buttress. Climb over an overhang (piton) to the right, loose and difficult (crux), easing off and then steepening to a groove. Belay 6 m below where the groove steepens. Climb up for 5 m and traverse right for 6 m to gain a crack system (#5 chock with no sling left in place). Climb the crack system (5.8) and belay where it eases. Continue up and left on a loose ridge (5.5), which becomes easier near the top. Descend to the south via an easy screed ridge that leads to the Minnewanka Valley.

MOUNT AYLMER - EAST RIDGE

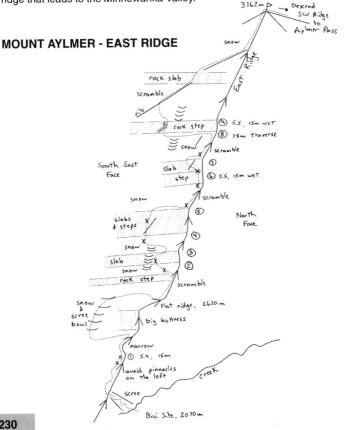

Mt. Aylmer

Mount Aylmer (3,162 m, 10,375 ft.)

Mount Aylmer is the highest peak in the entire Banff region. It dominates the view to the west when you turn the corner into the North Ghost Valley near the Silver-Tongued Devil Crag. From this vantage, especially in winter or early summer, the east ridge is a particularly striking line. A popular hiking trail traverses the west side of the peak from Lake Minnewanka to Aylmer Pass and continues into Spectral Creek and the Ghost River valley. Aylmer Pass is best reached from the Banff end of Lake Minnewanka and is 13.5 km with 810 m of elevation gain from the Minnewanka parking lot. From the pass, a straightforward scree scramble leads to the summit, which was first climbed in 1889 by J. J. McArthur. (*CAJ Volume 10, page 32*)

*East Ridge alpine grade III, 5.5
M. Siska & P. O'Byrne, June 1994

The first ascent of this route came in mid-June when the lower-angled sections of the ridge were covered in snow. A later climb will undoubtedly find more scree ledges and dryer conditions (take water!), which may permit more direct variations on the ridge crest proper. Neither time seems more recommended over the other, it is simply a matter of preferences. If you go early to mid-season expect snowy, wet conditions and a certain amount of avalanche hazard—plan accordingly.

Approach

The first ascent team used a combination of biking and hiking to reach Aylmer Pass from Banff and continued into the upper reaches of Spectral Creek. They then traversed the north side of the peak on goat trails to a "lovely kettle lake" (GR 099888) and then headed down to a grassy bivi spot at 2,070 m (GR 106875). This approach took 9 hours. A slightly quicker approach may be from the Ghost River valley but it is untried. The base of the east ridge lies some 15 km west of the Silver-Tongued Devil Crag. The topo opposite and description were taken from the *Canadian Alpine Journal Volume 78, 199, page 82*.

Alpine Rock

From the bivi, ascend a brown scree slope to gain the ridge crest. A scramble and half a pitch of 5.4 leads to the base of a big buttress. Avoid the buttress by traversing left to a big snow and scree bowl, rejoining the ridge at a long, flat bench above the buttress at 2,620 m. Here the fun climbing begins. The ridge consists of a series of rock steps and snow slopes on the southeast face, intersecting with a huge cliff on the north face. The route climbs up short rock bands and stays on the ridge or within half a rope length of the southeast face for a total of eight pitches (5.5). A compact 10 m step is reached high on the ridge. Traverse left for 75 m to a weakness in the step that forms the final difficulties. Above the step, ascend a rib to regain the ridge for the final stretch to the summit. The first ascent took 14 hours from the bivi. Descend by following the regular route on the southwest slope down to Aylmer Pass.

Devil's Head

Alpine Rock

Devil's Head (2,997 m, 9,174 ft.)

This impressive block-shaped tower is a prominent feature on the Rockies skyline and guided early travellers to the route west through Devil's Gap. The first ascent came in 1925 when the legendary Edward Feuz Jr. guided two guests to the summit via the west ridge. The ridge is relatively easy by modern standards (some 5th class) but it is long and Feuz's time of 5.5 hours up from a camp at 1,670 m in the Ghost River (4.5 hours down) remains an impressive effort and is rarely improved upon even today. (*Alpine Journal, London, Volume 38, page 67*)

The imposing east face presents a much greater challenge and has been climbed only once to date. The face is broken by a large corner system that is easily seen, especially in cross-lighting, from a considerable distance away. The route "Devil's Bargain" follows the corner system and gives an excellent, exposed climb on generally good rock. The position in the upper part of the route is reported to be exceptional.

Approach

The normal approach to Devil's Head is from the southwest and begins where a major drainage called Malamute Valley joins the Ghost River from the north (GR 198865). Malamute Valley is about 6 km upstream from the "North Ghost" parking area below Sentinel Crag and a 4WD or mountain bike is required to follow the "road" through a series of river crossings and washouts. Hike up the drainage for a short distance and then cut up right onto a steep hillside that turns into a open rib higher up. The rib leads north toward the west ridge of Devil's Head and gives a long but easy approach. A shorter alternative is to begin at a smaller drainage on the north side of the river between the "Alberta Jam" and "Sunset Boulevard" crags (GR 228867) and about 2.5 km from the "North Ghost" parking. The drainage comes out of a small canyon that looks impassable higher up but can be climbed on its west side near the mouth. The east face of Devil's Head can be seen in profile above the head of the canyon on the left. Walk up the drainage for about one kilometre and then angle up and back left to avoid cliff bands across a steep, wooded hillside. About 500 m higher an open rib is gained that can be followed easily to the base of the tower.

Descent

Scramble down the west ridge (some rappels—be sure to pay homage to Mr. Fuez as you rappel the sections he climbed up and down with little or no belay) and descend either of the two approach options described above.

*Devil's Bargain 305 m, 5.9

T. Jones & B. Gross, July 1984

The climb follows the corner system for much of the way and moves out right onto an exposed edge in the upper section. Pitons are recommended.

1 - 2. 100 m, 5.6. Climb a series of short steps to a chimney where the corner system narrows.

3. 40 m, 5.7. Continue up the chimney to a good ledge at the base of a steep section.

Alpine Rock

4. 45 m, 5.9. This excellent pitch follows a crack system on the right wall that leads up to a 3 m diameter cave (The Eagle's Eyrie).

5. 40 m, 5.8. Move right and follow a diagonal line of short cracks and overlaps to the base of a steep corner/crack about 15 m right of the main corner system.

6. 40 m, 5.8. Climb the crack to the top of a very exposed pinnacle that overlooks the main east face. Continue up easier and looser terrain to a terrace belay.

7. 40 m, 5.6. Easy but exposed climbing leads to the summit platform.

Poltergeist Peak (2,970 m, 9,700 ft.)

Poltergeist Peak is the unofficial name of the complex peak that forms the west side of Malamute Valley. To the north it is joined to Peak 2975 West (see below) by a long ridge that involves several other summits that may not be climbed.

Several approach options exist including various eastern spurs that drop steeply from the southeast ridge into Malamute Valley. The first ascent team of M. Benn and T. W. Swaddle (June 1970) started in the Ghost River valley and followed a smaller drainage due south of the summit (GR 165868) into a cirque. From the cirque, they made the long climb up slopes to the east to gain the southeast ridge where "it terminates above a big, east-facing cliff band." The summit ridge was gained through an "ice-choked chimney (easier later in year)." Descent was pretty much via the same route, 9 hours return.

Castle Rock (2975 m, 9,700 ft.)

Northwest of Devil's Head there are many unnamed and rarely climbed mountains with numerous peaks exceeding 2,900 m (9,500 ft). They form the headwaters of Waiparous Creek and in the past have been accessed via that drainage. See page 215 for access. Castle Rock is the unofficial name for a complicated peak that has several distinct summits of a similar elevation and ring the southwest corner of Waiparous Creek.

A large drainage west of Devil's Head called Malamute Valley drains south into the Ghost River and may give access to a variety of these peaks and possibly some good new routes. The Ghost River Wilderness boundary lies just west of Malamute Valley so it may be possible to drive to near the entrance to the valley. See the approach description for Devil's Head on page 233.

The descriptions listed here are taken directly from *Rocky Mountains of Canada South* pages 432-33 in combination with the original reports from the Canadian Alpine Journal (CAJ). They appear to be the most interesting of the lot and we hope their inclusion here will rise them from the depths of "out-of-printism" and foster some exploration of this rugged, scenic and overlooked portion of the range.

Alpine Rock

Castle Rock East (Peak 2975)
Northeast Ridge and Traverse, 5.5
E. Grassman & J. Rokne, Aug. 1967

This climb came as part of an impressive tour-de-force that traversed several unclimbed peaks to the west and northwest. It was part of a large ACC camp in the area in August 1967. Castle Rock East lies 4 km northwest of Devil's Head. It is the southeastmost peak of a group ringing the head of Waiparous Creek.

From a camp at the junction of upper Waiparous Creek and a southern tributary at 1,800 m (approximate GR 209953) follow the south tributary then mount the northeast ridge of the peak. Follow the ridge to a rock band at 2,680 m that circumvents the north and east side of the mountain. Move left and climb rock to the left of a steep gully, then climb the upper part of the gully (three pitches up to 5.5) to the upper ridge, then to summit (GR 180919), 6 hours.

Descend to the west and scramble up Castle Rock West (GR 161923), some 2 km to the west, 2.5 hours. Continue to the northwest to Peak 2942 (GR 148932) almost directly at the head of Waiparous Creek. The party had to backtrack a considerable distance to circumvent a deep, wide notch on the ridge. A traverse was then made west of the ridge, then ascended easy slopes to the summit.

Cumbersome slopes made the descent to the northwest of Peak 2942 time consuming with a bivouac required in the cliffs below the col. Finish descent into Waiparous Creek. (CAJ Volume 51, page 211)

Peaks 2910 & Peak 2940

North of Peak 2942 there are three more summits that complete the ring at the headwaters of Waiparous Creek. Two peaks with the elevation of roughly 2,910 m (GR 141947 & 144953) dot the landscape while a larger Peak 2940 lies to the northeast (GR 155961). The middle of the three (Peak 2910) was climbed as part of the ACC camp in Waiparous Creek. The party of K. Kubinski, P. Lancaster and L. Guy ascended the southeast ridge. The key to the climb was a hidden chimney through a low cliff band, 10 hours return trip.

The obvious challenge found in these peaks would be a continuation of the Grassman/ Rokne traverse all the way around the main Waiparous drainage to create a grand horseshoe that would begin and end in roughly the same spot in Waiparous Creek (GR 220943). Check it out on map sheet 82-0/6.

INDEX

Achilles 119

Acorn-er 41

Addam's Family 104

Alberta Jam 199

Allahu Akbar 137

Almond, The 48

ALPINE ROCK 227

An Arctic Arachnide 51

ANTI-GHOST, THE 223

Arms Race 133

Arrowhead, The 64

Aylmer, Mount 231

Back in the Saddle 63

Bandidos 122

Banshee 86

Bastion Wall 208

Batman Kicks Ass 125

Big Ass 137

Big Rock Traditonal 70

Big Willy 174

Black Hole, The 167

Black Mango 183

Black Strap 34

Blade Runner 64

Bluebell Corner 225

Bluebell Crack 225

Bluebell Extension 225

Boldly Go 72

Bonanza 77

Bonanza Area 75

Bonanza Direct 78

Border Bluffs 118

Border Rat 122

Borderline Buttress 119

Borderline Offwidth 112

Born to Chimney 48

Boundary Value Problem 112

Bowl, The 169

Boy Wonder 125

Buddha Belly 186

Caspar 169

Castle Rock 234

Cathedral Steps 122

Centrefold 183

Checkpoint 122

Chicken Heart 176

Chicken on the Way 175

Chimera, The 121

Chinook 225

City View 226

Cling of the Spiderman 127

Coconut 53

Compressor Fumes 270

Concord 216

Consolation 178

Costigan's Boil 229

Costigan, Mount 229

Countdown 175

Crack-A-Jack 167

Creamed Cheese 95

Creeping Senility 183

Cryin' Mercy 73

Cyclops 190

Déja-Vu 188

DEVIL'S GAP 35

Devil's Bargain 233

Devil's Eye 207

Devil's Head 232

236

Index

Diagonal	186
Diawl	121
Direct Finish (Consolation)	179
Dirty Dancing	162
Dog's Life	186
Double Trouble	115
Dreams of Verdon	66
Dreefree	102
Drip Route, The	32
Duveinafees	193
Early Morning Light	142
East Bay (Kolbassa Wall)	140
East Planters Wall	47
East Ridge (Mt. Aylmer)	231
Edge Clinger	133
Epitaph Wall	95
Feeling Groovy	186
Finger, The	218
First Movement	41
Fool's Gold	70
Freshest Sausages in the Valley, The	140
Fun Yet?	220
Gateway	174
GHOST VALLEY RIVER	145
Ghost Buster	104
Ghost Town Blues	81
Golden Cherub	220
Grey Ghost	86
Grey Ghost Wall	83
Grooves, The	130
Groucher's Corner	115
Gunslingers in Paradise	66
Gutbuster	216
Haemorrhoid	155
Handiwork	225
Handle, The	226
Hangover	175
Haystack, The	129
Helmet Crack	83
Hi Ho Silver	64
Hoods in the Woods	205
Hoss	57
How the West was Won	66
If You Love Her, Buy Her a Gun	140
Imbroglio	133
Italian Stallion	133
Jeff's Route	175
Ju-Jube	117
Kemp Shield	69
Koala Springs	187
Kobold Crack	102
Kolbassa Wall	136
Larry, Curly & Mo	209
Last Mango in Paradise	186
Leprechaun	211
Lethal Weapon	133
Little Bo-Peep	132
Little Gem	187
Loki	212
Lord of the Flies	131
Lucky for Some	209
Lugey's Copter	209
Macadamia	51
Mantissa	87
Maya	104
Menagerie	187
Mental Physics	133
Midlife Crisis	130

Index

MINNEWANKA VALLEY (see Devil's Gap)
Minou 183
Monster Mash 190
Montana Buttress 147
Moondance 160
More Dirty Dancing.............................. 162
Morning Glory Tower 142
Motocross Crack 225
Needle, The 132
NORTH GHOST 194
North Phantom Crag 154
North Side (Vanishing Point) 157
Nutcracker Sweet 41
Nuts and Bolts 43
Ockham's Razor 137
Old Style 121
On the Border 121
One Small Mouse 193
ORIENT POINT 31
Original Start (Montana Buttress) 151
Peak 2910 235
Peanut Dogleg 43
Peanut, The 32
Pecan Pump 53
Phantom Bluffs 116
Phantom Cracks 112
Phantom Crag Summits 228
Phantom Tower, East Face 113
Phantom Tower, South Face 110
Pinup 183
Pinnacle Chimney 165
Pinto Wall 220
Place of Dead Roads, The 104
Planters Valley 37

Poltergeist 104
Poltergeist Peak 234
Ponderosa Left 57
Ponderosa Right 55
Popeye 127
Priapism 171
Prickly Fear 186
Prosopopoeia 99
Psychokinetic 104
Quabalah, The 104
Rabid Crack 205
Recky Route 200
Revelations 121
Rhydd 121
Right End, The (North Phantom Crag) 159
Rise and Shine 142
Rock Doctor 66
Rock n'Robin 75
Rodents' Arête 170
Satan 211
Scaremonger 72
Scar, The... 38
Second Movement 42
Sentinel Bluff 183
Sentinel Cliff 182
Sentinel Crag 188
Separated Reality, The 167
Short but Sweet 128
Shred 70
Silver-Tongued Devil Crag 203
Skylark 187
Snake's Tongue, The 169
Softly Softly 186
Solar Winds 64

Index

Solitaire 130
South End (Planters Valley) 43
South Face (Kolbassa Wall) 137
South Face (Phantom Tower) 110
South Phantom Crags 147
South Side (Vanishing Point) 157
Southwest Ridge (Phantom Tower) .. 110
Southern Exposure 89
Spectre Crag 55
Spectre's Knife 58
Spirit Pillar 102
Spooks 161
Static Cling 187
Streaker, The 155
Stretcher Case 183
Strong Bow 121
Sugar and Spice 128
Sugar Loaf, The 128
Sunrise Wall 216
Sunset Boulevard 195
Super Heroes Top Rope 125
Super Heroes Tower 123
Supercrack 115
Supernatural 102
Superwoman's Wildest Dreams 127
Surprise, The 187
Teenage Wastland 130
Texas Peapod, The 113
Third Movement 42
Thor 211
Thunder God Buttress 229
Thunder Thigh Crack 202

Tough Trip Through Paradise 149
Tradesman's Entrance 72
Travellin' Light 119
Tuesday Afternoon 122
Twinkle Toes 186
Upspirits 102
User Friendly 72
Vanishing Point 157
Vision Quest 64
Vuja-Dé 190
WAIPAROUS CREEK 215
Waiparous Tower 218
Wall Nut 45
Wanna Fly Like Superman 127
Waste of Time 130
Wasted 130
West Phantom Crag 59
West Planters Wall 38
When Your'e This Big,
    They Call You Horse 140
Whispering Smith 160
Wild West Wall 63
Windmills of the Mind 92
Womb With A View 171
Wraith, The 107
Wully Canyon 170
Wully Sport 179
Wully Wall 172
Wully Watchers 179
Yo' Mama 137
Zephyr 85
Ziggurat 88

RMB GUIDEBOOKS

Selected Alpine Climbs in the Canadian Rockies
Sean Dougherty, 320p., $19.95
An up-to-date guide to the best mountaineering routes in the Canadian Rockies.

Sport Climbs in the Canadian Rockies
John Martin & Jon Jones, 272p., $20.95
Sport climbs in the Bow Valley west of Calgary.

Bow Valley Rock
Chris Perry & Joe Josephson. Due late 1997.
Multi-pitch climbs in the Bow Valley west of Calgary.

Banff Rock
Joe Josephson. Due spring 1998.
Rock climbs in the vicinity of Banff.

Scrambles in the Canadian Rockies
Alan Kane, 208p., $14.95
A guide to 102 non-technical peaks for mountain scramblers.

Waterfall Ice Climbs in the Canadian Rockies
Joe Josephson, 272p., $19.95
A wide selection of ice climbs on both sides of the Canadian Rockies.

Avalanche Safety for Skiers and Climbers
Tony Daffern, 192p., $14.95
Addresses recognition of avalanche terrain, stability evaluation and good routefinding.

Summits and Icefields
Chic Scott, 304p., $15.95
Alpine ski tours in the Rockies and Columbia mountains of western Canada.

To order, write or fax to:
Rocky Mountain Books, #4 Spruce Centre SW
Calgary, Alberta T3C 3B3, Canada
Fax: 403-249-2968, Tel: 403-249-9490
If you live in western USA or Canada phone **1-800-566-3336**
Visit our web site at: **http://www.rmbooks.com**